The Mushroom Doctor

The Wisdom Way of the Feminine Shaman

CAMILA MARTINEZ

Copyright © 2013 Camila Martinez

All rights reserved. No portion of this book except the brief review may be reproduced, stored in a retrieval system, or transmitted in any form or by any means—electronic, mechanical, photocopying, recording or otherwise—without the written permission of the author.

Contact: dakini@svn.net

Printed in the U.S.A. 2nd Edition 2015
1st Edition 2013

The names of some individuals in this book have been altered in deference to their desire for privacy. All photos taken by author except for the Tepantitla mural by Russ Beck.

ISBN-13: 978-069251087 2

DEDICATION

Above all, I dedicate this book to my meditation master, the Venerable Gyatrul Rinpoche, precious teacher and friend, who bestowed the blessings of Dzogchen on my spiritual path. I dedicate this book to the family of Doña Julieta, la familia Pereda Pineda. This Herstory is for my apprentices Deva, Terra and Devorah, excellent women. And to Tlakaelel, now in the Spirit world, Mexica-Tolteca Maestro and friend, who helped me see through ancient indigenous vision.

ACKNOWLEDGMENTS

Many years ago, in the beginning, my journey was witnessed by a wise woman elder, Ann Read, my gardening master, who encouraged me to write down my experiences. Very slowly over time the stories began to be written. It was like they had a timing all their own. She has passed on now, and to her spirit I give thanks.

Muchissimas gracias to Jimmy Zondowicz, fellow traveler and brother of the Nenes, for your great support, caring and daring on the journey.

Great thanks also to the familia Ramirez Garcia of the Restaurante San Jose in San Jose del Pacifico, for their generosity, protection, love and belief in my work. Thanks to Pati and Alejandro and the rest of the equipo at Temazcalli, in Puerto Escondido, Oaxaca, whose friendship, support, and healing over the years has been my joy.

Many thanks to fellow traveler, Maestro Tomas Filsinger, Nene extraordinaire, who continues to inspire me through his ancient vision and awesome art.

Thanks especially to Tomás Pinkson, Janine Canan, Devorah Joy Plotkin-Walder, and Leila Castle for urging me on at the end of this lengthy process. Muchas gracias Leila for your editing advice. A great wave of gratitude to Jessy Duterte and Michele McCoskey for help birthing the book and many kindnesses, Penny Van Dyk for inspirational service and being-ness, Denise and Robin Lai, C. Jay Bradbury, Renie Vazquez, Linda Dale, George Cisneros,

Steven Marshank, Deidre Goldberg, Mitchell Frangadakis, Richard Schwindt, Tripura and Om Anand, M.B. Brangan, Jim Heddle, Deva Luna and Terra Lee, so many thanks for all your kind support, knowledge, service, love, and for being there.

Gratitude of the heart to the magical appearance of Kelly Bradford and Barbara Goodwin with whose kind effort this 2nd edition was made possible.

A great mil gracias to Marion R. Weber, a precious inspirational luminous filament in this great visionary weaving for all the many kindnesses and love.

Map of Central Mexico with the Mazatec region shown in relation to Mexico City, the city of Oaxaca and Veracruz

The All-Seeing Eyes – Tehuacán, Puebla mural

CONTENTS

	FORWARD	xiii
	INTRODUCTION	xv
1	GIFTS OF UNKNOWN THINGS	1
2	WHERE THE TRAIL BEGINS	5
3	BORN IN THE REGION OF MYSTERY	11
4	THE INTERSECTION OF TWO WORLDS	15
5	COUNTING TIME	21
6	LA PALABRA – THE WORD	25
7	VENTURING OUT FOR BREAD	29
8	THE ENCHANTED SPRING	31
9	LAS COMADRES	35
10	THE MEDICINE OF LIQUOR	39
11	THE IMPORTANCE OF FIRE	43
12	WASTE NOTHING	49

13	THE NENES	53
14	HOUSE MAGIC	59
15	THE BLACK REBOZO	65
16	TÍO JOAQUIN AND THE NAGUAL	69
17	THE SOUND OF RUSHING WATER	73
18	THE MAGIC BEANS	79
19	CROSSING PATHS WITH THE GUIDE	89
20	TRUSTING THE JOURNEY	95
21	THE LITTLE WHITE SHOES	101
22	OUT OF MY COMFORT ZONE	109
23	THE MEDICINE WAY	115
24	FLIGHT OF THE SHAMANESS	121
25	IN THE PRESENCE OF THE SACRED	125
26	THE ALLY OF TOBACCO	129
27	THE EMBROIDERED HUIPIL	135
28	INEBRIATED WITH DEVOTION	139
29	THE GRINGO LEGACY	143

30	LAS CURACIONES – THE HEALINGS	153
31	RECONNECTING WITH THE ANCESTORS	157
32	THE JOURNEY NORTH	163
33	INCIDENT AT CHIMAYO	169
34	ENDURANCE COUNTS	177
35	RETURNING TO THE SIERRA	181
36	WHEN THE TRANSLATOR BECOMES THE TEACHER – CARRYING THE BULTO	187

FORWARD

It was a fortuitous day when my friend Ralph Metzner called to ask me if I would be willing to help sponsor an indigenous medicine woman from a small village in Oaxaca, Mexico on a first-time visit to the United States. Her name was Doña Julieta and she was a "curandera," a woman who heals with sacred plants and spiritual ceremony. I said "yes" which is how I met Camila Martinez who was to become a lifelong friend and amiga on the Good Red Road working to integrate indigenous spirituality and wisdom into the challenges of 21st century life. Camila had been studying with Doña Julieta for many years and would accompany her on her sojourn to "el norte" (north of the border of Mexico) helping to set up her public presentations and serving as translator. I knew from our initial phone conversation that Camila was a person of power herself and that a doorway had been opened to meeting not just one medicine woman but two!

A few weeks later I met Camila and Doña Julieta in person when they arrived in Northern California where I live. I was delighted to find that not only were they wisdom women of power and service in the world, they also shared a delightful sense of humor and zest for enjoying life. Over the next several weeks to come I was fortunate to spend time with them as they worked with a vast variety of folks who showed up to experience the healing shamanic ways of the ancient Mazatec people of Mexico passed through generations. Readers are fortunate as well for in reading Camila's book you too will learn from and about Doña Julieta's healing ways. In an entertaining adventure story you will hear about how Camila first met Doña Julieta and her many amazing experiences living with her in the small village far up in the mountains where people still followed the way of their ancestors living in harmony with nature and the spirit of the land.

Camila pulls no punches in her truth-telling about what she saw and learned about during her apprenticeship making sure to bring forth the wisdom teachings that are relevant to our lives and challenges we all face in the world today no matter where we live or what our spiritual path may be. We are all connected in a sacred web of life. We have forgotten how to live in respectful harmony and balance with that sustains healthy life for future generations. This book brings light to a path of return to right relationship learning from a wisdom elder and a wisdom culture offering guidance, insight and action pathways to once again unlock the love in our hearts to healthy living with all our relations.

So sit back on your favorite comfort chair and drop into a world of mystery, a world of magic and a world of wonder, part of our human heritage from south of the border that will have you turning the pages excitedly seeking what is next. Thank you Camila for taking the time to write this book and thank you to Doña Julieta, for your generous offering of your self and your wisdom ways, humble always, but so deeply touching of the heart and soul.

–Dr. Tom Pinkson
Huichol mara'akame
June 17, 2013

INTRODUCTION

The year, 2012. Where, northern California. A luminous light cord emanates from the vast sacred mushroom queendom in the high sierra of Oaxaca, Mexico. Ancient rhythms stirred in the ocean of consciousness, remembering Her essence, the Goddess, Creative Intelligence of the Universe of Universes. Invoking Her name and diving into the sacred lore of this land, the oral tradition between cultures is bridged. Creatress, all the sublime art of Nature speaks to me your essence. You teach me through your body, your sacred mushrooms, borne from your flesh, through alchemy of thunder and lightening.

Anáhuac, Aztlán, Mexico (mé-she-co), this land of California was, is still, and always will be a part of Mexico. Here is contained a great spiritual legacy, held energetically by Mt. Tamalpais, Mt. Shasta and the other great peaks. Here the Earth still holds many mysteries and secrets. It is the land of magic, miracles, and sacred places. Where coyote, mountain lion, and black bear roam, along with the spirits of Jaime de Angulo and Jack Kerouac. Lest we not forget, it is a place of deep power, palpable in places like Big Sur and the Point Reyes peninsula.

Our closest neighbor south of the present border of barbed wire fences and walls lies Mexico. Land of native people who have inherited the legacy of a sacred way of being, governed by entheogenic emissaries of other realms and dimensions, a country which slumbers under modernization. A great cosmic self-organizing thought, expressed in fungi, cactus and other plants that grow only in very special places on our planet Earth, grow here. Known to the natives, but to few outsiders, these plant allies illuminate the inner self with ancient cosmic knowledge.

This story is in veneration of the sacred mushroom teachers, the other precious plant teachers, and an extra-ordinary guide. It is a transmission of a way of healing, a way of Being, quite unknown to the outside world. It is a sacred story, lovingly covered by a silk rebozo with the dreams of the ancestors, the star travelers.

We are now one of the ripples of the ripple effect of the morphogenic field. Set into motion by the ancients we respond as their shoots moving in harmony with the energetic frequency deeply embedded in our consciousness, like a Call and Response song. The more we expand in trust with our antennae stretched, receiving the higher frequencies, moving on the energy wave, we integrate with an open secret.

Only by internally flying, self-liberation, are we allowed to view the Abyss, or a Black Hole, as a portal into a new region of the universe. In the Hindu vision, we live in the microcosm of Shiva's dance in our consciousness, burning up all obstacles, and knowing all is impermanent and in change.

When we put ourselves in the resonance field of places of power, such as mountains, pyramids, waters, or in the jungle, we receive transmissions of the Earth and spirits there. It is that energetic transmission that our awareness responds to. The ancestors spark us to think like pyramid builders. Paying attention, we begin with ceremony. We are called to dream, to conjure, to connect and re-connect, to study and to seek council from the remaining wise ones.

The airplane is our spaceship now. It gets us into the energy field of these lands blessed by the ancestors' wisdom, to ask for direction, as they did. We participate in an evolutionary quantum leap into the ancient future.

Our task is to nurture our seed in the most loving way and bloom. Now there is a planetary Awakening happening, and this story is for you dear reader, seeker. Some seeds only sprout after being in a big fire. It is that sacred consciousness that moves us now with great velocity to protect our Earth Mother. Let the love of HER awaken all of us to action. Looking within we see the holy work to be done. Fuerza! Strength to you, beautiful Cosmic flower.

Fiel en memoria
April 2013
Oxlajuj Baktun
Oxi' Akabal
Northern California

CHAPTER 1 GIFTS OF UNKNOWN THINGS

All stories have a beginning, but unusual stories sometimes have a remarkable start. It was one of those things that in retrospect, it was destiny. The Way opened to a deep current of wisdom. Initiation of the unimagined kind…when it's time it's time.

There I was, one of a small group of students imported from the barrio college of East Los Angeles to one of the happening west coast schools, the University of California at Santa Cruz. It was a new campus, and they were searching the academic corners to turn up students of color to manifest their multi-cultural vision.

Who would have guessed that my studies at the University of California Santa Cruz, in the early seventies would have provided the chance of a lifetime. The campus was a happening place in those days, with many big name professors. The "City on a Hill" as UCSC is called, was a totally foreign and unknown world. Northern California was dawning as a new reality for me. I was thrust into an intense academic scene. My main interest shifted to Anthropology.

The school was a magnet for the cutting edge and eclectic, international, and multicultural. I was at home, mostly because there was so much redwood forest on the land of the campus. I took solace in wild nature all around me.

I was there on scholarship, studying Anthropology, and slowly meeting students of other ethnicities. There were only a handful of us who had made it that far. UCSC was an educational opportunity afforded to a small number of students of color. But for me, it was another kind of education.

During my time at the university, I came across Ginsberg, Huxley, Schultes, Hoffman, Owsley, Leary, Alpert, and the unfolding list of those telling us to tune in, turn on, and drop out. I was in the perfect location. North of Santa Cruz about an hour and a half is San Francisco, and the full on psychedelic scene was happening there. Lots of students from school went up for counterculture action, especially taking in the Grateful Dead concerts.

There was a lot of acid happening at UCSC, and the whole gamut of experimental possibilities, including organics. We were a large university of experimenters. Actually one could look at UCSC in those days more like a big lab.

It was inevitable that my path would cross with LSD. I was sitting deep in a redwood forest and there was shown the secret world of plants and insects. My interests turned to the plant world, and human's native connection with healing plants and ways. I changed my major, and was guided to go deeper into the level of plant spirit medicine. Once decided, the plants took over.

Guided to the opportunity to try the "magic mushrooms," I received my first embrace from those beings. It was from this that a series of life changing events would begin to unfold, and my path to be made clear.

There was a group of Latino and Native American students who banded together to organize some cultural activities. I became a part of that group. It was because of this connection with the native grapevine that we got word that some indigenous elders were coming from Mexico, traveling with their students, to schools and reservations in the United States. We decided to host them the best we could, and make food for them. We were all so poor at the time. All we could do is offer beans and rice and floor space to sleep on.

One thing you cannot take away from the people is magic. And the Native Americans had it. None of us in our small group at the University had any idea who we were about to receive. A group of about twelve people, traveling in an old Blue Bird school bus, arrived on campus. Out came three adults and the rest, nine young boys aged ten to fourteen.

It is important to note that at that time few were paying attention to Native American elders at all. It was the time that the Medicine people began to go on the road to bring their teachings to the white communities.

A couple, who were taking care of the students, were obviously their teachers. And also another man, supposedly from a northeastern tribe, who for a long while took these people around the country to different native communities. Much later it came out that this man was a CIA operative, spying on native communities. Even at that time, everything was being observed by the government. Entering into indigenous reality meant opening my eyes in ways they had not been opened before. My middle class reality was shattered by the stories of the suffering of the Native American people. The best part of my undergraduate education was my first encounter with an authentic indigenous Master who gave me the first teachings on la Mexicanidad.

There I had a direct introduction to an unknown concept in the encyclopedia of Euro based academia, la Mexicanidad. Meaning You Are the Cosmos, la Mexicanidad is an ancient philosophical system, which includes knowledge transmitted through contact with beings of higher cosmic intelligence, Star Beings. These ideas were not a part of the Anthropology I was studying. However, the knowledge of this continent and the indigenous wisdom was something I was thirsty for. Several years later, this led to meeting my teacher, Doña Julieta.

My meeting with Maestro Tlakaelel, and his wife, Yetlanezi, keepers of the Mexica tradition, changed my life. They were masters of Nahuatl song and dance, and cosmology. We were walking at the farm at UCSC, and they invited me to come and visit their traditional native school, the Kalpulli Coacalco, in the state of Mexico.

I knew that this was the call of the spirit to come south to the land of my ancestors for the encounter of my life path. There was no way of knowing that my connection with Mexico, both ancient and modern, would deepen over the years, with countless trips to apprentice and practice traditional native medicine.

CHAPTER 2 WHERE THE TRAIL BEGINS

  I decided to travel to Mexico after I graduated from UCSC along with two friends from school. We made the journey in an old VW bus. It was a great way to see the country. We traveled all summer, down the East Coast through to Mexico City, and down to Oaxaca, Chiapas, and the Yucatan Peninsula, coming north up the west coast along the Pacific.

  Mexico City, today the largest metropolis on earth, continues in the legacy of the greatest indigenous capital of North America, Tenochtitlán (ten-osh-teet-LAN). It was the great ceremonial center, in a lake, a gathering place and crossroads of the ancient Mexica (may-SHE-ka) empire. Called Aztecs by the invading Spaniards, the Mexica, to this day are large populations within Mexico, a cultural continuum of many ancient spiritual practices. When Cortés and his army viewed Tenochtitlán from the heights of the mountains that they had to cross to get into the great valley of Mexico, they gasped at its grandeur. They said that they were beholding a vision, so magnificent were the buildings, roads, pyramids and ceremonial sites.

  Tenochtitlán was built on some raised land in Lake Texcoco around 1325 A.D. It is important to note that there is evidence that the valley of Mexico was inhabited in much more ancient times, by a literate culture. Abundant wild fowl and fish were in the lake, and super foods such as algae were farmed and eaten. Fresh food was brought in from the floating gardens of Xochimilco (zo-chi-MIL-co). There were many songs and poetry expressed in the Nahuatl language spoken throughout the valley. The Mexica had deeply symbolic dances performed by hundreds and thousands of dancers in beautiful, colorful attire, in spaces designed architecturally for special acoustics. Mexico was and is a place of deep visions, tremendous energy, and very alive with magic.

    Mexico City, located in the central part of the country, is a great hub of activity. What happens there affects the whole republic. It is the capital. This place, because it is a place of great gathering, is one of the great crossroads of the Americas. Always this is the place where the trail begins. Easy to fly into, and leave shortly thereafter, it is another energy field, very different then anything conceptual. Ancient and marvelous, with unending fascinating places to poke around in, Mexico City always has something magical to bump into.

    The more time I spend there, the more gets revealed to me about the multi-layered facade of the city. It never fails that I am drawn to the heart of the great metropolis. The *zócalo* -central square - is a veritable fountain of energy. Containing the remnants of the great ceremonial center of Tenochtitlan, these temples remain as a silent hub of the city. Surrounding it are numerous buildings built in the sixteenth and seventeenth century. Obvious in its message of subjugation, the Metropolitan Cathedral was built right on top of the Temple of Quetzalcoatl (ket-zal-KOAT-el), the cosmic energy representing the highest consciousness. The name Quetzalcoatl means the Feathered Serpent. Here there are two large adjoining squares where many thousands of natives danced and celebrated. Still drumming and dancing goes on daily. Indigenous culture is still alive.

The search for higher consciousness is an integral part of the indigenous reality. It was the Spaniards that were the barbarians. The ruin and the wreck that they wrought from the beginning persist today. Their display of character was exhibited in the torture of the captured, bound last emperor Cuauhtémoc, (ku-au-TE-moc) burning his feet in a fire in front of his relatives. He was later murdered on the order of Cortés.

Cortés was first received cordially onto the shores of present day Vera Cruz. The Emperor Moctezuma had received seven profound signs regarding the arrival, including auguries from nature, and the resurrection of his dead sister. He thought it was the return of the Lord Quetzalcoatl, a divine emanation, fulfilling an ancient prophecy. The much awaited fulfillment of this prophecy said that Lord Quetzalcoatl, an illuminated Being who had once walked the Americas, would return, bringing his great light. It did not take long after the arrival that the indigenous people knew that Cortés was not divine. The trials of these native peoples, and the subsequent theft, rape, enslavement and pillage, never could destroy their incredible spiritual resilience. From ancient times the native people depended on their seers, their wise men and wise women.

They had societies devoted to cosmic consciousness. While Europe was in the Dark Ages, these descendants of the pyramid builders traveled inter-dimensionally. The use of power plants was employed for thousands of years. Archeological evidence gleaned from the carved mushroom stones are ancient, some which date from 1000 B.C.E.. With extensive knowledge of the arts, architecture, mathematics, calendrics, and astronomy, the civilizations of Mexico are nothing short of astounding.

Today in many parts of the United States, Mexicans who have long been settled here, as well as recent newcomers, are still considered as second class citizens. Taking on the most humble of labor for work, these people are the backbone of the labor force. It is on their hard manual labor that so many of the people live. The great agri-businesses, and service-oriented businesses are run on their backs. Mexicans contain the genetic roots of great civilizations, which will fortify them through time. It is this greatness, this Spirit, which is now awakening in the brown skinned masses, and it is the awakening of la Mexicanidad.

Oaxaca is the place that I resonated energetically with the most. It was love at first sight. And it was here that my fate was sealed. I was well received by the spirits of the ancients there. In the folds of the verdant Sierra Mazateca, I met my teacher, Doña Julieta, the Mushroom Doctor.

The colonial city of Oaxaca, the capital of the state, had sixteenth and seventeenth century buildings, an aura of peace, and a fine *zócalo* - central square- that was a great crossroads and meeting place for many shamans and healers. This was a place of magic. Long wooden slat benches beneath spreading shade trees made an ideal meeting place.

Oaxaca was a place with many indigenous people, with ancient cultures and customs, such as the Mixteca and Zapotecs. The different tribes were skilled at many kinds of exquisite handcrafts, such as weaving, ceramics and gold jewelry. The Mercado Benito Juárez was full of colorful handmade art, as well as delicious regional native food. Life was lively on the surrounding streets with many street vendors in their small stalls along the outside of the market. Aromas of barbecued meat filled the air, along with the wafting sounds of marimba music. Who could not be enchanted by all this?

Oaxaca is a large state with many kinds of climates, including deserts, mountains, fertile valleys, and the beautiful Pacific coast. People are courteous, modest, and friendly. Oaxaca is a sacred place on the Earth Mother's body. It is in Oaxaca, where the sacred cosmic knowledge of the ancients is alive and practiced, a living reliquary of a continued transmission. Oaxaca is a part of me, and I honor the holy earth there.

CHAPTER 3   BORN IN THE REGION OF MYSTERY

The word shaman, or feminizing the word, shamaness, is an anthropological term, claimed by many in these times. Doña Julieta was a true wise woman, a healer, a mediator between the worlds, an inter-dimensional traveler, a true cosmic citizen, a loving mother, knower of secrets, doctor, lawyer, cook extraordinaire, artist, and herbalist. There she was known as *sabia*, (a wise woman), shuta tshinea. She knew many people, and lived a humble life, in a remote mountain village, in the Sierra Mazateca, near Huautla de Jiménez, Oaxaca, Mexico.

Born in Huautla de Jiménez, of a mother who was renowned for her healing powers and curing through the sacred mushrooms, she idolized her. Her mother's name was Regina, and she came from a female lineage of healers. Doña Regina was a very independent woman. She had a *fonda*, a small food stand, on a dirt street in Huautla de Jiménez.

It was from her cooking that she supported her five children. She served the pack train drivers, who brought outside supplies from far Puebla, merchants and locals. There was little time for dealing with her small children, so the little ones were free to roam.

Doña Julieta was a shy child, and spent much time in a safe corner out of the way of many feet. From an early age she suffered great hardships. In the mid-1930's, her mother had many difficulties raising her children in this remote region. People came to Doña Regina for healings from far and wide. She was a well-known *curandera* in the region. It was in this environment that Doña Julieta was raised, watching her mother cook and perform healings. It was a full and demanding life. Reality was harsh.

Doña Julieta was the black sheep of the family. She was the youngest and the most vulnerable. Many times she told me that she was an orphan. In her mind, meaning really, without a mother or father, without true protection. When she was young, life was extremely tenuous. They were very poor.

Her earliest recollection of the sacred mushrooms was of being a very little girl, and one day early, someone had delivered some mushrooms to her mother in a box. Julieta was very hungry. Because her mother was busy, Julieta took the mushrooms and started to eat them unnoticed. After a little while, her mother discovered her, and asked her how many she had eaten. She didn't know. Doña Julieta said that she remembered that the mushrooms made her dance and dance.

High in the remote mountain village of Huautla de Jiménez, Oaxaca, existence was rudimentary for many. And up until the mid-1970's, in many of the areas in that region, the people were living in basic conditions, with very little access to material goods from the outside world, because of the great poverty. One thing that is important to understand is that the Sierra Mazateca is a very large region. There are people that live in the Sierra Mazateca, but cannot understand one another, because they speak distinct dialects of the Mazatec language. These dialects change from village to village in some areas. This was a remote place, very difficult to get into, an area that Cortés and his invaders never penetrated. The Sierra Mazateca was a natural geographical barrier. The culture was ancient and the spiritual realization of their wisdom holders was beyond concept of the Spanish invaders (and later outside European visitors).

The ancient culture of the Mazatecos stretches far into prehistory. The name Mazateco, or Mazatec, comes from *mazatl*, deer, a Nahuatl word. Mazateco means people of the deer. The Mazatecos were part of the Nonoalca, a tribal confederation that allied with the flowering spiritual civilization of the Toltecs to the north. The brilliance of their combined influence reached far south to the land of the Maya noted in the architectural and ceramic styles in some of the pre-Columbian sites.

CHAPTER 4   THE INTERSECTION OF TWO WORLDS

How utterly unexpected was the meeting with Doña Julieta. Arriving in Mexico City, a family member of my fellow travelers asked if we wanted to go to the region of the sacred mushrooms. We agreed, and left at night, traveling in an old VW bug. The road took us through Tehuacán, Puebla and then onto the large town of Teotitlán del Camino, Oaxaca at the foot of the mountains.

We drove through the abandoned streets, illuminated by a few light posts with bare bulbs, creating an eerie glow in the darkness. Four of us were traveling, and it was summer, the time of the rainy season. We drove up into the remote mountains, and not far from the village where we started there was a roadblock. Soldiers. Soldiers with guns. Our driver, luckily, was a savvy guy.

It was early a.m. and there were no vehicles on the road. Unknown to me, the region had been sealed off by the federal government. Only local natives could pass. Approaching the barricade, our driver told us to be quiet and let him do all the talking.

He was well able to deal with the soldiers. Unfriendly and gruff, the soldiers quickly changed their way, when our driver produced cigarettes and a copy of Playboy. Happy, they let us through. Waving at us as we passed, they were content with this recent windfall on their remote outpost. Boons were few in those parts.

It was wet, and the road, better called a track, snaked through the mountains. We drove for hours, with cascading waterfalls along the side of the road, spilling over the earth, creating much mud. The road was single lane most of the time, with a steep drop off on the driver's side. The big cargo trucks which carried out regional produce, and carried in supplies, created deep ruts in the road.

I was amazed at how this intrepid little Bug could travel so well over such bad roads. The car had to straddle the deep ruts filled with mud, made by big truck tires. Sometimes when the car had to enter the ruts, it was dicey traveling.

We got stuck in a light rain. Totally dark around us, the headlights dim in the vastness. Fortunately our driver came prepared and got out a shovel. The guys dug out the tires, threw rocks underneath, and pushed us out. Continuing, we bumped along for hours.

Traveling along the almost constant sound of the rushing waterfalls was present. We traveled slowly, and at times the clouds settled in over the road causing almost a complete white out. We traveled windows down to hear any oncoming vehicle.

What was on all of our minds was the big WHAT IF A TRUCK COMES ALONG and we have a head on collision. With no shoulders of the road to get off on, and visibility so low, we all were on edge. After what seemed a long while, the clouds started to lift. Now we could see a little way in front of us and the rain had stopped. And then, out of the fog emerged one big cargo truck. He saw us and hit the brakes. Miraculously, we were on a part of the road where it was wide enough for two vehicles to pass.

Few vehicles made it up into those mountains other than those cargo trucks. It was remote and lonely. A bad place to break down or have trouble. Before the time of trucks, it took muleteers four days to travel from Teotitlán up, bringing supplies into the region.

The people traveled these paths by foot.

The climb leveled off as we passed through a sleeping village with a few streetlights. From there the road started to descend. Winding down and down. Just at first light, we reached a river, where we stopped and got out.

The sound of the rushing water, the smell of the fresh dense foliage, a multitude of ferns dripping with water, and the sweetest bird song I have ever heard, made me feel I had entered an enchanted place. Everything was alive. Each of us felt this lovely energy. We all looked at each other and smiled, knowing that we had made it through the worst of it.

We got back in the car, and continued along the river, when the road abruptly started to climb. There was a big rockslide, produced by a spring running out of the mountain on one of the wide uphill curves. The Bug skirted the edge and we made it through. No big boulders came down fortunately. The road was bad from the rain with many holes. We slipped and slid, up and up, trying to maintain upward momentum.

Coming around a curve in the pre-dawn light, I had my first view of a Mazateco. In regional dress, his white cotton shirt and white loose pants at mid-calf, and cream colored straw hat gave him little protection against the cold. What was most striking was that he was a midget. Walking barefoot, he was joined by a woman, his same size. They were as amazed to see us as we were them.

We continued on, and no one was yet on the road. We entered the village, and parked. Walking a little way, we descended on a muddy path down to an old wooden door and knocked. It was chilly early that morning; the dampness of the earth from the night's rain penetrated our clothing. The sound of footsteps nearing from the inside, and the door opened, showing a smiling round face of an Indian woman.

A few words of greeting given and recognition of our driver opened the door to the patio. As we closed the door behind us, we entered into another world. We walked quietly single file across the dark brown earthen patio, into a small room, which was an eating area. Welcomed to sit down after the ten hour journey, we awaited Doña Julieta to appear.

It was early for visitors to arrive there. Nonetheless, soon thereafter, she crossed the patio to greet us. Joyful and smiling, she received us lovingly into her home. She was a vision. Tiny with long black hair, and black flashing eyes, she surveyed each of us. We must have looked a bit like refugees in our rough and mud splattered clothes.

The room was simply furnished with hard wooden chairs, and a small wooden table that sat six squeezed in. In one corner, a table for kitchen supplies, and next to it a large black clay olla, pot, with drinking water.

Very soon, Chavela, who had received us at the door, brought us steaming hot cups of black coffee. Grown by the family, and laced with raw brown cane sugar and cinnamon, it was delicious. Conversation flowed about our adventure through the night getting there.

Without any asking, in a short while, plates of hot black beans and eggs, with big corn tortillas appeared in front of us. It was the first of many meals I would have at that table with Doña Julieta. She encouraged us to eat and attended us, going back and forth to the outside kitchen across the patio to bring more food. As we ate, Venancio, the man of the house, came to see who arrived.

Again, joyful recognition, and a warm welcome for all of us. Shortly thereafter, the children of the house came in smiling. There were seven children, each very lively. We met them all and they lost no time making friends with us.

We made room for the children to eat before heading off to school. The house was in constant motion. It was still overcast with low clouds, preventing us from seeing what was out there, beyond.

After the children were tended and had left for school, we had time to talk more story. We were the first American outsiders that they had met, and my first encounter with an authentic medicine woman.

This was also my first experience of native hospitality. Although the surroundings were very humble, we were made to feel at home. In her way, she smilingly asked, "How long can you stay with us?" I reflected on the culture where I came from, where the question usually went, "When are you going?"

We did not have a fixed time in mind to stay, and this said, all was well. The space allotted to us was on the second floor, in a room used to store large bags of coffee, and other supplies. We camped on the floor in our sleeping bags.

Our time spent there was mostly within the family compound. We did do some hiking around the village, but kept a low profile. I spent a lot of time with Doña Julieta around her fire as she cooked. It seemed like a good part of her day was taken up cooking for the family. The hidden jewel was Chavela helping to do a lot of the chores.

The next day, it cleared. Early morning the silence was pierced by roosters crowing in the distance. Arising I went out onto the porch and saw the exquisite expanse of emerald vegetation extending into all directions, with the mountain close behind us. The small village was in the vicinity. Early, the aroma of wood fires penetrated the air, making me hungry.

Days passed and time seemed suspended. Stories were told, clothes washed and dried, and the rain set in again. It was rainy season, which in southern Mexico happens generally between May and September. The rains at times were torrential. The patio became muddy and wooden boards were put down to walk on to avoid the puddles.

There was a big secret happening up in that region especially in the summer time. The rains brought the sacred mushrooms out. It was a time of healing ceremonies using this precious medicine. In this loving household, I was to experience initiation and apprenticeship into the healing ways of the sacred mushrooms under the guidance of Doña Julieta.

CHAPTER 5 COUNTING TIME

The Sierra Mazateca was a land of no time. Nestled in the lap of Mother Nature's lush and verdant skirt, life was governed by the forces of nature, the world of daylight, as well as the world of darkness. There was a rhythm governed by the earth that the villagers lived by. This cosmic rhythm determined the daily and ceremonial life of the Mazatecos.

The daily rhythm worked with the light, beginning before daybreak. At high noon Doña Julieta would say, "The Great Lord is on His throne." This was a major time marker in the day, for certain rituals and healings had to be done just at the height of the sun's power.

In Doña Julieta's house when healings were happening, before mid-day was a busy time. All the herbs and elements had to be gathered and prepared, ready for the right moment. The outdoor earth patio had the house built around it in such a way that no one outside the family compound could see inside. It was perfect for doing healing work, especially for burning large quantities of copal in the open air.

As dusk fell, the villagers went inside. Night came, and at times great fluctuations of energy went through the house. Early in my time with Doña Julieta, there was little electricity that had reached the remote villages. So we would sit under a bare light bulb, in a room with walls made of stone, open to the elements on one side, no door or window in their spaces. When there was no electricity that room became magic in the candlelight. Time was passed telling stories. Sometimes we sang and danced. The children would be attentive and their ingenuity added to the family entertainment. Doña Julieta would sing beautifully in Mazateco. There was a lot of joy and love in the house.

Night time took on another aura when ceremonial medicine work was being done with the sacred mushrooms. The entire family in some way was part of the healing. As part of the household I witnessed the condition of the patients, many who had come from very far, desperate for spiritual and physical healing.

These traditional healing ceremonies are called *veladas*, and are exceedingly rare for an outsider to encounter. Being in all night ceremonies required tremendous energy. Accompanying Doña Julieta was like being with a force of nature.

At night the street was empty out front, as were the rest of the few village streets. In those parts the natives believe that the spirits walk at night. The people do not go out unless necessary. Night is a time when sorcery is practiced. Like chickens being enclosed to roost the door from the patio to the outside world was closed as night fell, secured by a *tranca*, a stout pole wedged into the ground and against the door. Locks were not used.

Time was measured by no time. Rather there were cycles of nature that marked time. It was the calendar of nature that the Mazatecos followed. The traditional Mazatec calendar is made up of nineteen time frames. The elders read signs in nature that told them when to proceed with the ceremonies that were a continuum throughout the annual agricultural cycle. The stars were read and the combined knowledge of over a thousand years of observation gave the indicators of the beginning of the sacred cycle of the corn.

Everything revolved around the planting and harvesting of the corn, coffee and honey. These were the main cash crops of the Mazatecos. There were times of the year when there was plenty, and then there were times of starvation for the humblest of the natives. It all revolved around land, if you had it, and if you did, how many local hired hands could be gotten to harvest the crop.

CHAPTER 6   LA PALABRA – THE WORD

La palabra (the word) has a special significance for people of an oral based culture. Before the sophistication of writing developed all there was, was the word. Even after writing developed it was not available to the masses, and so, what counted was *la palabra*.

A person was measured by their word. What they said, and doing what they said, was what counted. Keeping your word was of ultimate importance. The word was what held society together. When communication was by word of mouth, when all the cultural history was handed down orally, great value was placed on the word.

Commerce was carried on by the word. When a first price was given for a burro, and the back and forth haggling was done, it was all settled by the word. Many times the word would be accompanied by touch, a slight handshake. More like a touching of palms instead of the strong handclasp.

The word held the meaning of the power of truth. Cultures flowered through the word. In pre-Columbian indigenous cultures there were great poets like Nezahualcoyotl, king of Texcoco, and splendid orators. Oratory, or speech giving was an art, and much appreciated. These things exist to this day and are practiced in some schools.

Many of the great pre-Columbian cities were designed architecturally so that when the king or authority spoke to the public they stood in a special spot where the acoustics allowed throngs of people to hear. Today in places such as Teotihuacán you can experience this. Just clapping your hands in the right place resounds very far.

When truth was needed to be spoken an oath was sworn. In these times when are we called to give an oath? *La palabra* was important to express loyalty within the family and the culture. In all things you were only as good as your word. The majority of village people were honest and humble. It was unusual to come across anyone who would lie. And so when you came across a liar, they stuck out and it seemed like an offense.

Having gone through western education, and then winding up in the village, it became painfully aware to me how so much of speaking the truth was lost in the land of my birth. And so, the lesson of giving and keeping the word was of ultimate importance. Giving your word, looking someone in the eye, face to face, was what bound people together.

After many years some people from the outside world slowly filtered into Doña Julieta's house for healing. I had many experiences with these people who were mostly from Mexico City. She called them *acelerados* (accelerated or fast paced). Usually they were on nervous overload from their lifestyles and were crying for help. Some were drug addicts, having fallen prey to cocaine in *la vida loca* (the crazy life) in the city. When their time came for their ceremonies with the sacred mushrooms many were fearful. Doña Julieta was always so kind and reassuring. These people worked out the energetic knots in their systems like a spiritual gnashing of teeth. After hours of intensity on their own personal journey of transformation, each one came out healed.

Sometimes people from the outside would show up on weekends.

One never knew how many ill people were going to arrive. Since there were no accommodations in the village everyone stayed at the house.

For the very wealthy that somehow found their way, it was another world. In Doña Julieta's house comfort could not be bought; hard wooden straight-backed chairs, sleeping on the floor, and no heat. It was really tough in the cold summer rainy season.

One of the great delights was sitting in the kitchen that had only three complete walls, bathed in the elements, talking story late at night around the table. Doña Julieta and her husband were so hospitable to everyone. There was always a flow of delicious black coffee, big handmade tortillas, and black beans.

Speaking the truth honestly was paramount. Today there is much alteration to this very basic way of establishing trust between people. With the incursion of electronic devices now even *la palabra* becomes not only cheap but our language is altered. It leaves one to think about a basic conundrum: was this an opening up of new communication through these forms, or is it leading to real communication breakdown. When technology that has become mainstream separates people from speaking person to person, face to face, a breakdown occurs. This kind of separation is happening now.

In Mexica culture, it is told that our ancestors left us flowers and songs (*flores y cantos*). What beauty and inspiration comes from flowery speech and melodious voice! Just the tone heals you.

What beauty lies in the indigenous cultures where people greet strangers with "Good Morning," "Good Afternoon" and "Good Evening." A place where there are terms of respect and endearment spoken in daily relationship. Children were called lovingly *papacito* (little father), for the boys, and *mamacita* (little mother), *madre* (mother), or *madrecita* for the girls. A place where strangers wish you enjoyment for your food when they pass you, or when you are served. There is reciprocity in this word exchange. It makes you a human being. Having words with people and a meeting of the eyes creates contact. It is this direct contact which always has been the way of being human.

CHAPTER 7 VENTURING OUT FOR BREAD

Food was always an issue in the house. When there was just enough to feed the ten mouths of the family it became a stretch when guests or patients arrived. One evening soon after I got there Doña Julieta told me that there was not enough food for everyone.

Night had fallen and it was pitch black, no stars, and a great silence. The door to the patio had been secured for the evening. She called me over to her and said, "I need you to go out to buy bread. Be careful and hurry back."

With a few pesos on me, I went up the street flashlight in hand. The tiny *tienda* (store) was up the way not too far. I got to the door of the one room "store" and entered. There before me, in a rustic building of hand hewn pine planks, was a simple counter made of wood boards nailed together. Behind it the proprietor looked up surprised to see me.

The room was lit by candlelight, as there was no electricity. He had two things for sale. One was local bread, *pan salado* (salty bread), and the other was *aguardiente* (white lightning). The round loaves of bread were stacked up on a shelf behind the owner. I went up to the bar to ask for a loaf.

To my left were three local native men, bellied up to the bar, drinking shots. I was careful not to look at them so not to arouse attention. Before I could get my pesos out of my pocket, I felt a whoosh of energy, and I turned to look at these guys. The man next to me had keeled over backwards and hit the wooden floor like a sack of cement, out cold from the brew.

A squabble started and then, one of them landed a blow to another ones face. Then a fight broke out, drunks beating the heck out of each other. One had a machete in his hand. It was a scene out of the Wild West.

At that point I threw the pesos on the counter, grabbed the bread and ran out the door to the sound of them falling to the floor. Out on the dirt street, there was not one sound of a dog barking in the village. No one was out.

I walked back to the house with the bread in hand. Entering the patio I went to the kitchen and presented the bread. All the kids were happy to have bread to eat with their evening coffee. I told Doña Julieta what happened. She looked at me piercingly and said, "Now you know why I do not want you to go out alone, especially at night. Some of these people are savages." There were other reasons too, which in time she explained.

Within my own family, I was raised without restrictions. My schooling was heavily disciplined. And so, coming to a village in a remote corner of the mountains of Oaxaca and having restrictions regarding my movements was something new to me. However in this new land it was of utmost importance that I obey Doña Julieta's commands. I was to find out later that I needed protection. The foray out to get the freshly baked bread made it taste even better.

CHAPTER 8 THE ENCHANTED SPRING

The village where Doña Julieta lived was for the most part a quiet place located on the side of a lush and verdant mountain. There, banana trees grew near pine trees and colorful orchids lived in the pines. The steep mountains all around were a vast green carpet, stretching to the farthest visible distance. From her house other villages could be seen clinging to the sides of the folds of the earth.

The day began before dawn, starting to work immediately to grind the corn to make the tortillas for the family. This necessary work had to be completed first so that her husband would have food to take with him to the fields. After coffee and sweet local bread the men left for the long walk to the family plots of land down by the river, shortly after dawn. All the work was hard work, and in the springtime, because the sun became very hot at mid-day, the more difficult tasks were planned to be accomplished in the earlier, cooler part of the day.

Springtime is the time of clear blue skies and magnificent warm weather. It is a time of fullness of the earth, and she is rich in her bounty in the Sierra Mazateca. The mountains are busy with the activity of many Mazatecos working to hand harvest the exquisite coffee grown in the region. The coffee bushes, with their dark green leaves, had branches adorned ornately with the beautiful clusters of ripe red fruits, the coffee berries. These tall plants laden with red berries were an eye feast that made you happy just to see them. They gave a feeling of well-being and wealth. Coffee was the main cash crop of the region.

At the end of the day, when Venancio, Doña Julieta's husband, returned with the local people he employed to help with the harvest, he would offer them the customary *trago*. The *trago*, or alcoholic drink, of local preference was *aguardiente*, a close to 100 proof firewater made from sugar cane. *Aguardiente* is white lightning that can make you drunk in a blink. The Mazatecos have many uses for aguardiente, among which are ceremonial uses. It is commonly used at the end of the day, after hard physical work, as a relaxant and restorative for the health.

After a few *tragos*, the people's faces take on a noticeable relaxed glow, and the mixture of the days hard work of harvest accomplished, money on the horizon, and a mellow gathering blends for some fine storytelling. Everyone was sitting on a long wooden bench, all eyes cast on Venancio, as the mood struck him to tell me a family secret.

After a number of years I came to understand this story told to me by Doña Julieta's husband as dusk was falling. It had to do with a part of my training but in a very secret way that they didn't let me know about until many years later. It had to do with a special tree and a spring. During the very beginning of my apprenticeship it was very important that I had to drink water from a spring that went into her house, and so that was the water that I drank for years. The water came from an enchanted spring, located on land belonging to Venancio's father.

This story is connected with the name of that place. Names were given to places by the ancients to indicate what was in that place, or the properties, qualities, or attributes of that place. The village where they lived was situated amidst a great forest. It had a very peculiar name. The name came from the great Yoloxochitl tree that grew not far from the center of town. None of the natives in that region knew how that tree got there. It was a mystery. In all the surrounding forest there was not another one of its kind.

The mighty size of it showed that it was of great age. That tree was very interesting because the native stories said that it was about two lovers, a warrior and a beautiful woman. The warrior got killed, and the woman died of sorrow. Because of their great love, they were both reborn as parts of the same tree. He became the trunk and the leaves, and she the flowers.

Beneath its great roots, underground was an enchanted spring. Just below the tree there was a water tank into which the water flowed. From this tank the villagers collected water. At times there appeared a great serpent that arose out of the water and frightened everyone, causing the natives to drop their containers and run. The great serpent was the guardian of the spring. The sudden appearance of the great serpent when people were collecting water caused fright among the villagers. A meeting was called with the elders regarding what to do. After much discussion, it was decided to lure the serpent out of the water enough so that they could capture it and take it far away.

With this plan set, one day a group of village men gathered and laid in wait, out of sight of the water tank. Everyone was anxious for these indigenous Mazatecos lived in a world of magic and nature spirits. They greatly respected the power of this great serpent and did not want to anger or offend it. After a long wait the snake rose up, and as it came out of the water they grappled with this monstrous serpent. The men had constructed a big palanquin out of wood on which they could transport it. They captured the snake and placed it on the palanquin, tying the writhing mass to the stout wood. The brave men carried it out of the village on their shoulders, down the mountain. They took it to a distant part of the river which courses through the mountains, and that is the place where it still lives today.

The Yoloxochitl tree was in the vicinity of her house, and Doña Julieta's children and I would go to that tree from time to time. I would always be warned, "Do not stay long" when I went to the tree. Usually, I wouldn't be allowed to go out of the family compound frequently. I was kind of sequestered. I didn't realize it at the time, but I was being protected. At one point, Doña Julieta finally told me frankly, "There are a lot of *brujos* in this village." This meant both male and female. Also in the early years of my studies, it was illegal for any outsider to be in the village, so I had to be hidden. The region had been closed off to travel. When I escaped the compound for some kind of errand or other, then I would go up to the tree. The warning said that it was enchanted.

Old history in that region told that the *duendes*, the dwarves, would appear near that tree. There were also dwarves who lived by the spring under the great tree. It was the dwarves' water, and this tree was one of the entrances to their realm. Of the great magical happenings in the sierra were the activities of the *duendes*. These were not fairies they were dwarves, magical, inter-dimensional beings. These dwarves were known to abduct little children and sometimes men, to play with for days at a time. They also throw stones. But that is another story.

CHAPTER 9 LAS COMADRES

Life in the *sierra* was hard for women. The saving grace was the extended family of *comadres* and *compadres*. This system of *compadrazco* was a living flux of energy between people based on reciprocity. During a lifetime a family built up a network of *comadres* and *compadres*, assuring help when needed.

Your *comadres* were your back up, your work force, the ones you could depend on. Especially in times of *fiesta* when quantities of food had to be made by hand and cooked over fire, the *comadres* were invaluable. Everyone pitched in.

One of native communities' basic values is reciprocity. Giving to one another, selflessly, and providing some form of exchange when needed, was part of life. Everyone living in community knows how important it is to share and serve, especially your *compadres*. This fundamental idea of sharing the load in order to survive goes way back to the time when people were nomadic.

In fractured western society individuality was stressed. In native culture it was the group that worked together. I had to unlearn what I was taught in school and family; that proud and fierce individuality. Even beginning to think in terms of the group, instead of the self, was another way. It was not the American way. Fortunately, I could unlearn quick.

And so I was introduced to *comadre* Lupe and *comadre* Reina. *Comadre* Lupe was a quiet and humble person of middle age. She lived alone and had one son who lived outside of the *sierra*. Her salt and pepper hair lay in two braids against her back, tied together so not to disturb her work. Her dress was worn and she wore the mandatory apron, which caught most of the soot from the fire, and dirt. *Comadre* Lupe took care of many details of daily living around the kitchen, while Doña Julieta tended the many patients that came for healing to the house.

Many hours were spent with *comadre* Lupe preparing the food in the outdoor kitchen. I could always count on her for a gentle good-natured smile. She would laugh at me as I tried to pronounce Mazateco words after her. It was a tonal language and difficult to learn.

One of the best learning times was making *tamales* by hand. This took a long time and usually it was for *fiestas*. The house had seven children at home so there were many *fiestas*. The *mole tamales* were highly prized, as this is a regional epicurean delight.

Comadre Lupe also pitched in as part of the work force for the family when it came to coffee harvest time in the spring. This was very hard work, picking the coffee berries in the heat of the day with many biting bugs. At the end of the day everyone would gather on the patio before dispersing to their houses.

Sometimes as if by surprise, *comadre* Reina would appear at the lower portal to the patio before the sun got too high. She would be carrying supported by a tumpline on her head, a forty kilo load of freshly butchered meat. Her upper lip was sweaty under the weight and the heat of the sun. Her job was to walk through the mountains selling the meat off her back to people at their homes.

At that time this was a precious service as there were no markets nearby or fresh food readily available except for that which was grown in the family garden. Some basics such as tomatoes, chilies and onions were trucked up to the village periodically.

When *comadre* Reina visited, it was always a time to stop and drink coffee and get the news of what was happening in Huautla, the capital of the region, where she lived. It was several hours away by foot, up and down the steep mountains.

Comadre Reina was a kind person with a toothless smile, front teeth missing, which she hid behind her hand. She was beautiful, with long black braids, smooth brown skin, flashing black eyes, strong, independent, and fearless, walking alone in remote areas. Despite carrying her load of meat, she wore the most elegant dress made of shiny magenta satin. The picture of her was completed by a long *machete* carried in one of her hands. I enjoyed being around her, and I was a novelty. These people had no contact with anyone from the outside world.

CHAPTER 10   THE MEDICINE OF LIQUOR

Of the many remedies that are used by native healers in the Sierra Mazateca, *aguardiente*, made from distilled sugar cane is prominent in many cures. The indigenous people of the region were very poor, without money to buy medicines. However, *aguardiente*, ninety proof and above, was readily available and used as a medicine for many illnesses.

The vast majority of the Mazatecos enjoy *aguardiente*, the use and abuse thereof. Produced in the region, it is used ceremonially, as well as part of *remedios caseros*, which are home remedies. In the early seventies, *aguardiente* would be delivered to Doña Julieta's house, brought on the back of a native man who carried a very large heavy container of it secured by a tumpline to his head. In this ancient style of carrying, the elder walked the steep mountain trails from village to village, dispensing one of the main and simplest healing remedies.

Seeing this señor arriving at her house, laboring under the weight of his precious cargo, I mused that this was the original home delivery. After siphoning off his clear liquid treasure into the provided container, he would sit and rest awhile, himself taking a *trago*, a drink of *aguardiente*, to make him strong to endure the rest of his journey on foot through the mountains.

Sweet and hot, the *caña*, as it is called, would immediately affect your system with one shot. In healing, *aguardiente* is used by rubbing it onto the body, alone or with plant infusions. It is also used in *limpias*, the spiritual cleanses, in which the Mazatecos have great faith.

Customarily it is drunk by men and women at the days end of work in order to relax, and also when it is cold, to help them warm up. Alcohol abuse was one of the social problems of the village, leading to violence of various types. Fueled by *aguardiente*, many disputes were settled by *machete*, a sharp, long blade knife, used in daily work in the country. Deep body gashes were some of the emergencies that Doña Julieta attended to.

Part of my training was to learn how to drink liquor. I was not raised drinking liquor, and it held no charm for me. So this was another type of education. Doña Julieta told me that it was important to learn to drink liquor to help my energy.

I tried to get to know *aguardiente*, but it became quite impossible. It was just not my medicine. It was just too strong. Instead I was given *mezcal*, and from then on, I received many teachings on how to use this most amazing liquor. Made from distilling the agave plant this exquisite elixir is highly medicinal.

Slowly, through this introduction, I began to open to the spirit of Mayahuel, the spirit of *mezcal*. *Mezcal* production was done in another region of Oaxaca, and when this great gift arrived, it usually came in large five to ten liter jugs. I did not know it at the time, but a few years later, I was given a full initiation on the production and identification of *mezcal* (as there are many kinds) from my Tío Enedino, a Master of *mezcal*.

The agave plant is beautiful and of many sizes. The big ones have leaves, which are called *pencas*, some which are three to four feet long. The ends come to a point with a sharp needle like spine. These spines also are on the edge of the leaves, and so one has to be careful around the plants. In pre-Columbian times, indigenous people of Mexico and Central America used these spines for auto-sacrifice by piercing, inducing trance through blood letting. Of note, is that rulers performed auto-sacrifice publicly for the benefit of all and for the blessings of the Cosmos.

There was a whole cultural etiquette surrounding the use of liquor, both distilled and fermented. It is used in all ceremonies, births, deaths, illness, spirit possession, other healings, to seal a deal, celebrations, and settling disputes. It is a medium of serious exchange. And so I was to learn the Way.

At the bottom of this teaching was one simple law of observance with *mezcal*, respect. When one receives the teaching and applies it, it is highly beneficial. If you ignore the limit, there is a big price to pay. If you make the mistake of over indulgence, the best way to put this is that you feel like you are dying for about twenty-four hours thereafter. And nothing helps you. This harsh lesson only takes once to learn.

CHAPTER 11 THE IMPORTANCE OF FIRE

For most of the time, Doña Julieta taught me around her fire. Her kitchen was outdoors, with three walls made of hand hewn wood boards, and one open side, facing across the earthen patio to the rest of the house. Most native kitchens in this region are this way, separate.

There was a window cut through the wooden planks that made up the back wall. It looked out onto the verdant expanse of the mountains, with banana trees and tropical vegetation stretching far below. The kitchen was simple and austere.

The center of the home was the hearth, the place of fire. An essential element, fire, like woman is fire. Light and heat. Her fire was located on top of a mesa, a special table constructed to hold the fire. All cooking for many years was done over open fire.

Her family was large, and much of the day was taken up around the fire preparing food. Black beans made up a good part of their diet, as well as tortillas, and these both take a long time to cook. And so, much time was spent in the kitchen.

The most delicious simple foods were cooked there, and mostly were cooked in clay *ollas*, which were large black clay pots. The tortillas were cooked on a *comal*, a flat clay plate. Measuring about one foot across, the tortillas were made of the white or yellow corn that the family grew in their *milpa*, cornfield, down by the river. They were subsistence farmers and lived mostly from what their fields produced. They grew corn, beans, chilies and onions, the basics for survival. The cycle of the year surrounded the planting of the corn, and the harvest of the corn, coffee, and honey. The latter two being cash crops.

Village life was simple. Doña Julieta's house was a small four level enclosed *adobe* and stone compound, close to the center of town, built onto the side of the mountain. Most of her time was taken up by her daily family duties, and tending patients.

In the early seventies travel up to the *sierra* was very rough and difficult, so there were few outsiders that made it to her village. After the initial word got out about the region being the center of the sacred mushrooms, through the exposé done by Gordon Wasson in Life magazine in the mid-fifties, seekers started to find their way up to the capital, Huautla de Jimenez. It was fortunate that Doña Julieta's village was far away and out of that flow. She was a hidden jewel.

The fire was sacred to her, and so on a regular basis her husband would bring his burro or mule laden with wood from the *campo*, countryside, in the forest way below. For a very long time, she did not let me near her cooking fire. I could stand around it, warm my hands from the cold, but never tend it, or stir it. She was very particular about her fire.

The fire was kept going throughout the day, and when the cooking was finished, or temporarily suspended for a few hours, the wood would be slightly retired from the center so that it would not needlessly blaze away. Everything was conserved, even the wood for the fire. The smoldering wood was pulled away, just a little way from the center, to keep the coals burning so that the fire could quickly be restarted at a moments notice.

These were women's teachings, centered around the fire. For a number of years when I began to apprentice with her, my task was to peel the garlic, peel the onions, and wash the tomatoes. That is all she would allow me to do. So I knew my task and daily, sometimes more than once I did this. Most of the food that she made contained these basic ingredients. Then after I graduated from that task, she let me dice the garlic, cut the onions and the tomatoes.

Once after returning north to the States, I saw how the Italians did the garlic, putting the whole unpeeled clove under the flat part of a big knife, and smashing the garlic in order to peel it easier. The next time at her house, I proceeded to do the garlic that way and she adamantly told me not to do that, and to peel it whole. Each woman has her way. It had to do with the integrity of the clove. Not smashing it, or mashing it. It had to be whole.

Her kitchen was very smoky at times, thus the reason for the absence of one wall. When the firewood was not totally dry, since there, the rainy season lasted many months during the summer, it always smoked. When she cooked, and the wind played with her, she had to move around the fire to get out of the smoke to stir the pot. On those days, cooking involved a lot of squinting of the eyes. And also getting smoked.

I became the food runner, taking the cooked food from the outdoor kitchen across the patio into the other kitchen where everyone ate in shifts at a small table that accommodated four people or maybe six squeezed in. With so many children, Doña Julieta usually ate last. It was her pause in a long day of constant work.

She impressed upon me the importance of the fire, telling me that it would advise her of visitors. There was divination done by fire also, to find out the cause of serious illnesses of patients. A white rock was used, and after a *limpia* was done with it, it was placed in the fire. The fire would change the form of the rock and indicate what illness the patient had. This kind of divination was done for spirit disease.

In that region also, divination was done by reading the flame of candles. Candles were used in *limpias* for healing. In the early days tallow candles were used. But the best candles were made of pure white bees wax. These candles were highly prized and expensive.

Part of living sustainably was having your own beehives, which yielded honey, pollen, and wax. The honey was coffee honey, with the hives located among the coffee trees. When the honey harvest was happening, everyone was happy. Part of the combs of honey were brought to the house and everyone delighted sucking on them and chewing the wax.

In Oaxaca among the different native tribes, special pure yellow bees wax candles were made with beautiful adornments for certain fiestas. Big luscious candles that weighed a lot, some three to four feet tall and six inches in circumference, with colorful paper flowers placed into the wax, made exquisite offerings on family altars. When lit they burned for many days, emitting a delightful healing smell.

The fire from the kitchen also produced charcoal, which was used for heating in an *anafre*, or small open stove made of metal. This was used during the rainy season to provide some small heat to ward off the cold of the mountains. The charcoal was also used to grill meat, especially *tasajo*, thin cut slabs of semi-dried salted beef. This was a delicious delicacy only eaten once in awhile, since meat was costly and not easy to get. Few people had cattle and there was no market in the village.

Ash from the fire was also a valuable asset. It was used to clean pots and dishes instead of soap. Used along with lemons, it cleaned any oil off the plates, pans or *ollas*, and did not cost a thing. Wood ash was also used as a medicine and also for cooking certain foods. It was also added to the compost.

The fire produced many valuable products and was held as sacred and kept in a certain way. At night Doña Julieta would put the fire to sleep, speaking to it and arranging sticks or wooden spoons in geometric forms on top of it. This was the magic of fire, and once when I asked her husband about it, all he would say about her was, "*Es su misterio*" (It is her mystery), or her mysterious ways.

CHAPTER 12   WASTE NOTHING

What stories the bare wooden walls of the outdoor kitchen could tell. It was the place where all kinds of news, gossip and teachings happened. The kitchen was a place of hard work, a woman's place.

For the size of the family, the kitchen was quite bare of supplies. The rustic shelves and worktables, dark brown from wood smoke and aged by use, held the basic tools. The *mano* and *metate* (the grinding stone and pestle), ancient and made of heavy gray basalt stone, was the center of it all. Intimately connected with grinding corn, sacred to the people, each woman had her own.

Allied with this, were several clay *comals* (concave flat clay platters) of different sizes. After grinding the corn, the tortillas were made by hand, and then cooked over the fire on the *comal*. Oaxaca is famous for it's tortillas. About ten inches to a foot across, some even bigger, and perfectly round, they are the host (as in communion) to native people.

Just outside on the patio was a waist high tree stump which had been driven into the ground and served as the base of the hand crank metal coffee grinder. When it came time to do the grinding it was Chavelita or *comadre* Lupe who performed this ancient task. This was hard work.

In the kitchen on the board shelves were a few jars with dried herbs in them. From the eaves hung a large cluster of green bananas ripening. The shelves were dirty and needed some attention. So I decided to take on the task of cleaning the shelves.

On this afternoon, no one was around except Doña Julieta and myself. I was in the kitchen alone, with dust cloth in hand to begin the cleaning job. As I dusted, I saw small woven baskets holding some of the dry things like onions and chilies. Moving things around, I noticed that here and there, there were pieces of dried onion, and pieces of dried chili, lying on the shelf.

I gathered the bits, and put them near a pile of dirt and debris on the table. It did not take me long to complete that task which left me covered in ash dust and soot. On the table was a bag of black beans, which I was to clean.

When people of other cultures speak of gourmet food, in the sierra of Oaxaca, the indigenous people eat gourmet native food. At the top of the list, are black beans, along with handmade tortillas. In order to make good beans, the first step is cleaning them.

Cleaning the beans is a holy task, because the wellness of the family depends on the sharp eye of the cook. Small stones, hard dirtballs, and plant stems had to be taken out of the beans. When the family consumes two kilos of beans a day that is a lot of bean cleaning.

I sat on the wood floor of the kitchen with my feet on the dirt patio in the shade, slowly and methodically cleaning the beans. I tossed all the little stones and other trash onto the patio, including many misshapen, shriveled, and bug bitten beans, which did not look good. When I was almost finished, Doña Julieta walked across the earthen floor towards me.

"What are you doing?" she said, looking at me strangely. "Cleaning the beans, Mamita!" She looked down at my feet at the pile of debris. "Don't throw these beans away. I save them." She gave me a little container and I began to pick out the bean remnants.

She surveyed the kitchen clean up, and noticed my little pile of dust and trash on the table. Pointing to the dehydrated pieces of chili and onion, she said, "Don't throw these away." My mind was suspended without looking for a possible reason.

Leaving the wordless space open, she proceeded to tell me that in the winter, there are times when mothers come to her begging for food. These people were starving. And so, all the little beans that were deemed unfit for the meal, were put aside for just this time.

The women were given these remnants, so that when cooked, they had a broth to drink. She went on to tell me that at times she had no money and little food, then, these small pieces of dried onion and chili were brought out to cook with. Coming from a place where there always was food, this was my introduction to what hunger meant.

I noticed that in the household there was a chain of consumption. Everything got consumed. What the humans did not consume, the dog, turkeys, pig, or compost got.

As I gathered the tiny pieces of onion and chili from my debris pile, I asked her where she wanted me to put them. She indicated a place on the shelf, in a jar. Before I could go any further, she looked at me with her piercing dark brown eyes and said, "*Hija* (daughter), waste nothing."

Then and there was the beginning of a focused mental spotlight on not wasting. If you practice waste nothing, then it is a good introduction into the give away. When you practice the give away, even beginning small and then getting big and bigger, then you are blessed by practicing generosity. When you practice generosity, you slowly loose attachment to things. Losing attachment to things lets you give away more, wasting nothing. Through this practice, you gain many blessings.

Thus, the kitchen transmission.

CHAPTER 13   THE NENES

In the many years at Doña Julieta's house, there were few outsiders that came. In the course of my time there, several from distant Mexico City arrived. They were all young men, around my age. Who knows how they got there in the beginning. All were adventurers.

Since the *adobe* house was basic, with little extra space, we all had to make do with sleeping arrangements where we could. We all slept on the floor on woven palm mats. It was cold, especially during rainy season.

I was encouraged to go on outings with the boys, up to the market in Huautla on Saturdays to buy necessary supplies. There was little to be had in the village so we went in the car they came in. Transport was difficult in general as there basically was none, when guests arrived from afar with a vehicle, a market run was in order.

Going to Huautla was always an adventure. You never knew what was going to happen on the road. From the village, the road wound down, mud and rock, slick where springs ran across. Reaching the river below, we crossed on an old bridge. Stopping there, we got out, and walked, being absorbed by the dense nature around us.

There was a palpable special energy in that place. It was in the sound of the rushing water and the smell of the plants. It was in the song of the *jilgero* bird, which chortled melodiously, echoing in the forest. An air of magic.

Doña Julieta always impressed upon me that the Earth was alive. After receiving her teachings, this word, alive, was not a concept, but a palpable reality. There was expression, communication, reception and transmission. These include auguries from the movement of insects, the flight of birds, animal sounds, cloud movements, and celestial phenomena.

The Huautla market was lively and colorful. Local ladies in colorful dress and those from nearby villages strung lines and hung beautifully embroidered *huipiles* (traditional native dress) and textiles for sale. Local produce of vegetables and fruits, spices, sugar cane, and *aguardiente* (white lightning) were sold. Native people from all over the region came. The men were in traditional white *calzones* (pants) and cream-colored hand woven palm hats, either bare foot or with sandals. Not much Spanish was heard in the streets. The people spoke Mazateco. Huautla was the regional capital, and it bustled with life on market day.

We stood out in the market, obviously not from there. It was good to take care of buying early in the day, because by mid-day, the heat sometimes was intense. We split up, each taking part of the shopping list. The market became like a scavenger hunt. Agreeing to meet at the vehicle, we took off on foot.

It is impossible to go to market without eating your way through. So many delicious fruits, juice, tacos, and *tasajo* (barbecued meat). The vendors were offering samples. Unusual native foods, such as baked *maguey* (agave), *chapulines* (roasted grasshoppers), and wild mushrooms were consumed. Another world of food opened up, and it was native food. I became an aficionado.

When going to market, we cannot forget the *borrachos* (the drunks). The *borrachos* were laid out on the sides of the streets adjacent to the market. Gone to the world, these people sometimes had walked for many hours to get to Huautla for market day. After doing business, they got into drinking *aguardiente*, and then after one too many, they were truly shitfaced. They were part of the whole picture. The people just moved around them.

After wading through the crowd of bodies about my size, I noticed among the smiling faces that the people tended to like to have gold teeth. One or two, and sometimes more. These made their smiles even more shining. Against the rich brown of the Mazateco's skin, the charm was irresistible.

On the return journey, bumping along the road filled with potholes, made the travel slow. Seeing more of the region, we could appreciate the altitude and varieties of microclimates. It was lush and green, with many flowers. Climbing up from the river you could see the distant villages, some only reachable by foot. It was a beautiful place.

Returning to the house in the late afternoon, we came bearing all kinds of goodies, including sweet bread for Sunday morning coffee. The house was peaceful as usual, with patients coming and going. Somehow amidst all this, the house chores got done.

The *Nenes* (babies), as Doña Julieta called us, were her joy. She doted on us. Her hospitality was magnanimous. Seeing her pull off giant meals over a wood fire was astounding. With little provisions she created a feast. We all were most nourished by the large tortillas made from the corn Venancio grew. They were delicious, served with black beans hot from the *olla* (clay pot), a fried egg, and coffee, black and aromatic, sweetened by raw cane sugar and cinnamon.

The boys came from well off families in Mexico City. Some were spoiled by their privileged life. Others were jewels in the rough. Doña Julieta loved us all.

Of the boys who came, as it turned out, each had his own genius. Doña Julieta, recognizing this, nurtured each one with her love. She was doctor and lawyer, counselor and spiritual guide. Years down the road, one became an author, one a hotelier, one a car dealer owner, one an eco-tourism company owner, and one a major artist. Each applying the lessons learned from the medicine, and the loving guidance of Doña Julieta. The last two are still my friends; our unique experience a deep bond.

In the course of these surprising encounters with the boys, Doña Julieta at times allowed some of her children to accompany us to escape the confines of the household compound. Once, two of the boys decided to bring several of their friends with them on their journey to the mountains. There were five of them, one a woman.

The day after they arrived, we all decided to go down to the river for some refreshment, and one of the kids, Hippie, came with us. Doña Julieta pointedly told me to take care of him. We were all by the river, in a place where it was not too wide but flowing fast. I had told the group to watch out for the child.

Hippie was one of my favorites of the children. A radiant little face, and a humble character, he was entirely loving and innocent. He was around five years old. I decided to go downstream a bit and sit apart from the others who were talking a lot disturbing the natural ambience. City folk. Suddenly, I heard a scream, and my attention was drawn toward the river to see Hippie being carried away by the current. He was wading and had fallen in. He was sputtering and going under, not able to swim.

I leapt up and jumped in the water just in time to grab him as he was being swept along. I hauled him out of the current, choking, onto the bank. Instead of crying, he was standing silently, blinking and shivering. I had nothing to cover him with to warm him. He was in shock. I held him and we walked back to the others. I was so angry with them for not paying attention to the child because they were so wrapped up in themselves. I yelled at them. We quickly scrambled to leave.

When we got back to the house, Hippie's clothes were still wet. I told Doña Julieta what had happened. She immediately took him and did a *limpia* (spiritual cleanse) on him. This was my first case of *susto* (fright-shock) that I got to see healed. The traditional native medicine that Doña Julieta practiced taught through direct experience. Here my training began in the use of eggs. Certain eggs have been used in native medicine to heal the body. The training in learning this art of reading eggs takes a long time. As is custom learning this kind of medicine, you learn by practice as the situation arises.

The *Nenes* came to the *sierra* to trip on the sacred mushrooms, and she was our Cosmic Mother, the Mushroom Doctor. The ceremonies were held at night. The house quieted down and the surrounding village also, as darkness fell. The door on the patio was closed and secured, and there, amidst children and family, voyagers were ushered into other realms. This was a house of spirits. This was a house of healing.

Windows to other worlds opened with the smell of burning copal and prayers said by candlelight. Watching her do the invocation, holding a burning white candle, with closed eyes and raised hand with open palm, she called on the energy of *Todo Poderoso* (All Powerful) and the Virgin of Guadalupe (Tonantzin), and a litany of Protectors.

The children of the family were integrated into the experience.

From the earliest age, they were used to taking the sacred mushrooms. Then, as the *Nenes* came, the children were there as our protectors, watching over us, and taking care of us. More than once they were there for me, acting as a buffer against unwanted energetic interference.

In the early days, somehow word reached some outside people in Huautla that I was at the house. We were tending to the days chores when a young man arrived. He said he had walked from Huautla several hours away. He was Mexican, university age, and educated.

When inquiry was made why he came, he said he came to see me. We conversed, and it got late. Too late for him to make it back before dark. And so, he was allowed to spend the night. There was only one place to sleep, and that was in the same room, a storeroom, where I was bedded down on the floor.

Time for bed came, and Doña Julieta called two of the children to come with me to sleep close. In this way, the children served to protect me. Another occasion when I was on the medicine, an intense situation arose, with a distant family member who was visiting, not knowing what my state was, got in my face. The children came around me and guided me upstairs to a quiet and protected place.

CHAPTER 14 HOUSE MAGIC

People look at houses like they are things, inanimate, solid. I learned to see a house in a whole different light at Doña Julieta's. Her house, made of *adobe* (handmade clay bricks), clay tiles, stone and cement, seemed to be a living entity. So much happened there, so many healings, so much drama, so much family life, joys and sorrows.

The house was permeated by magic. It was inhabited by many spirits. It was there that I got my initiation to house magic, how to maintain a house and the spirits therein, and how to defend it when the situation arose. Since pre-Columbian times copal resin was burned as a main defense against illness, spirits, and bad energy.

Of the many interesting things on Doña Julieta's patio, there was something that caught my eye amidst the plants. The concrete stairs, which led from the patio up to the second level was lined with different kinds of plants in containers both on the bare earth and on the steps. Colorful lilies, red roses, and purple orchids brightened up the patio. Underneath the steps was an area used as a storage area.

On one of the gray pillars was a hummingbird hanging upside down. Its emerald feathers fading. Who knows how long it had been there. Curious, I decided to ask Doña Julieta about the hummingbird.

There are many birds in the *sierra*, and the hummingbirds have a special significance. In this case, the explanation opened up another way of looking at things. I was to learn about love magic.

In the culture that I came from love and romance were looked at differently. Here in the sierra love was a serious endeavor, involving intermediaries, matchmakers, sometimes lengthy courtship, and of course bride price. There was besides this, an alternative to all the aforementioned, and that was elopement. Of course to save face, the family of the bride would claim that their daughter had been stolen, "*La robaron.*"

Entering into an engagement was serious business. It entailed agreements between the parents of the couple, drinks, and exchange of gifts. These formalities were to secure the ties between the couple and the families. Within the formality of marriage, a house was formed. And this house would shelter a family. It was the presence of the hummingbird that kept the ties firm. Its presence was a visual reminder of all of this.

As a living entity, the house spirits had to be fed. This was a daily activity, carried out at the altar, with candles and prayer. This was a holy house, a place of deep healing. From the altar, the prayers carried over into the kitchen. The main elemental conduit was the fire. A lit flame of a candle, or a cooking fire, were the transmitters.

The elements were strong in the *sierra*. Not long after I had stayed with the family for a period of time a big earthquake happened collapsing the upper two stories of the house. It was very difficult for everyone. Three rooms on the first floor patio level were still inhabitable, so the whole family piled into one room to sleep. I slept with all the kids, like sardines, on the earth, on a woven palm mat, with a large foam mat. When I first arrived after the quake as a pilgrim I was saddened by what I saw. It was devastating for the family. There was no money for rebuilding. It took years to recover. However, recover they did, slowly slowly.

When the house was being reconstructed, and the second floor more or less completed, I spent time away from the main action in the to be completed kitchen area where it was quiet. It had been turned into a bedroom, complete with bed, which was a real luxury. The new reconstruction was much more solid. There was a bathroom down the walkway, around which was a narrow continuation, a ledge where I often sat in solitude, meditating and praying.

In the summer months rainy season, the weather was intense. Sometimes it would rain for days on end. Cold and damp, sometimes encased in fog, the village took on a mysterious air. At times you could not see up the road because the fog was so thick.

One late afternoon Doña Julieta told me that a big storm was coming. She was entirely in tune with Mother Nature and could read signs in nature. She made sure that we all ate early and that the kitchen had been secured before darkness fell.

It seemed sudden. A huge storm came and broke right over us. All the kids ran for cover. Big roaring winds swept through. I was up on the second level, and when I came out of my room, I looked over the railing to the patio below to see her working with the elements. She had set out an *anafre* with live coals on the earth, and was standing in the howling wind and pelting rain, burning something with a big odor. Hair flying looking primal, she raised her voice to the wind, arms to the sky, praying in Mazateco. Sparks from the *anafre* were flying in many directions consumed by the darkness. It seemed that the wind took a form and whirled around her.

All I could do was watch in amazement. It was as if she was

possessed. She was in communication with the wind. I was witnessing something that had always been, the medicine woman's direct connection to nature, and the ability to pacify or command the elements.

After a short while, the wind died down, the storm passed and the danger to the village, and our household was over. This was the first time that I had seen the ability to command the elements. I would see this many more times with other blessed people.

The next day dawned clear, and I asked Doña Julieta about controlling the wind. She told me that certain spirits ride on the wind. Some malevolent, such as the ones that blow down the cornfield. Another class of spirits, which travel on winds, are those which carry certain diseases. When the spirits are fed, they are pacified. This was the beginning of learning to feed the spirits.

The commanding of elements is one of the gifts that are used to protect the house. It is a necessary magic to know. The house having its own life was in expansion. In the rebuilding, at street level on the second floor, a reception area was under construction. A makeshift roof of corrugated metal over timbers, and walled off to the street, the room had a dirt floor with piles of gravel in the corners.

One evening we were sitting down in the kitchen. The night was cold and foggy. All was silent in the village; only the sounds of the household were heard. It was a night with mystery in the air. Suddenly there was a sound of something like glass breaking up on the street. Soon thereafter a rock hit the tin roof of the second floor. Odd, I thought, where could a rock come from? We all looked at each other. After a few moments, another rock hit the roof. Looking at her daughter and me, Doña Julieta lost no time in ordering us to come with her, as she started to sprint up the stairs. We ran after her and caught up to her in the semi-darkness of the doorway into the reception room. She motioned to us for silence. We stood motionless, like cats, listening. Again another stone hit the roof.

Someone was out there. The three of us entered the room. She started to chant in low tones, and then suddenly turning to us she said, "Quick, pee in your hand!" Pee in my hand? Huh?

Faster than lightning, before I could think or say anything, I followed suit and dropped my drawers in unison with them and we all were there stooped over peeing in our hands. As soon as we had our handful, she commanded, "Now throw it in the corners!" And told us what to say.

Trying to complete the casting of our urine without hitting one another and making our mark in the dim light, acting swiftly while she chanted on, was a sight to see. We focused on the pee. Throwing tendrils of energy out, casting out the harmful forces just outside the walls, the chant went on and finally stopped.

Again we waited in silence. After awhile, there were no more stones on the roof. We retired for the night. The next morning, when Venancio went up to inspect what had happened, he found that someone had broken the side view mirror on their old truck. As is usual, not all *curanderas* are well looked upon. Not everyone in the village was friendly.

CHAPTER 15   THE BLACK REBOZO

There was only one store in the village, which was owned by Tio Lolo. Maybe it was because he was probably the richest man in town, or his character, but just about everybody hated him. He was one of those guys who, when you walked into his store, he began to undress you with his eyes. Lascivious and leering, he was to be avoided at all costs.

His store had dry goods, beans, rice, corn, canned goods, and other general store items. It was hard cash only, something that many of the villagers did not have. He loved money and would do any kind of business to get it. Tio Lolo, because of his wealth, had bought a big red cargo truck to bring supplies purchased in Puebla back to the village.

He drank a lot, which inflamed his character even more. Loud and a braggart, sometimes he grabbed women who came into the store. He was known by the locals as a *sin verguenza* (a person with no shame). I was not asked often to go to the store, and if I had to go, some of the kids usually accompanied me.

Next to the store was a *molino* (a mill) where daily the village women covered by their traditional black *rebozos* (shawl) took their *nixtamal* (cooked corn for tortillas) to be ground. For a few pesos you could have a kilo or more of corn ground, cutting through much labor bent over a *metate* (grinding stone).

On a quiet village day, someone came running into Doña Julieta's calling her to come and help in an emergency. She had been in her kitchen preparing food, with a knife in her hand, and quickly took off running. Down at the *molino* a crowd had formed at the door and Doña Julieta pushed her way in.

Before her, a horrific scene. The woman, who had been gathering her *nixtamal* from the *molino*, had gotten her *rebozo* caught in the machine. Wound around her neck tightly, she was strangling. A bunch of women were gathered around her paralyzed in terror at what they were witnessing, unable to do anything.

Her face was turning blue, eyes bulging, when Doña Julieta shoved the gawkers out of the way to get to her. Without a moment to lose, her knife still in hand, she began to cut the tightly wound *rebozo* from the woman's neck. Working furiously, she cut through the densely woven cloth, the sharp knife going into her neck. Blood poured profusely as the woman was freed, unconscious. Quickly Doña Julieta staunched the blood flow. The woman slowly regained consciousness, and her life was saved.

Awhile after this incident, word came that Tio Lolo was missing. He had gone with his chauffeur, who was also his bodyguard, in his big red truck to buy merchandise in Puebla. A search party was sent to find him. Venancio went along. Much time passed, and then they found the place where the truck had gone off the road.

It was steep and a long way down. Nobody wanted to endanger themselves to retrieve the body. Venancio, who was Tio Lolo's cousin, was the only one that took on the task. In a heroic act, Venancio completed his strenuous effort. Tio Lolo was found murdered, shot by his chauffeur. The killer was never found. These instances of robbery and murder were not uncommon. It is said that the kind of death that you have reflects the kind of life you have lived. For this unfortunate man, this was surely the case.

The black *rebozo*, which was for such a long time an essential garment for indigenous women, slowly became left out of daily wear. As time passed, even in the capital of Oaxaca city, many women from the surrounding regions stopped wearing the *rebozo*. Elegant and charming, this multi use fringed hand woven cloth was being left aside, only worn by older women or at *fiestas* (parties).

It is still a favorite garment of mine. Soft from over thirty years wear, it is a luxurious fabric, lightweight and warm, carrying the beauty of the weaver, and a wonderful soothing energy. The waning use of the black *rebozo* was another sign of the big change coming to the people.

CHAPTER 16 TIO JOAQUIN AND THE NAGUAL

One of the great pleasures of life in the village was to receive visitors. At Doña Julieta's house, because of the geography of the mountains, friends who visited were few. Contact with the outside world, the world beyond the mountains was scarce. Mexico City was a planet away.

There was no transportation in between villages, other than by foot. Throughout the rugged Sierra Mazateca, are footpaths etched by native feet. In some places the paths are narrow and precipitous, skirting the mountains, and in other places wide enough to accommodate two mules side by side.

For more than a thousand years, these footpaths provided the thoroughfare for trade and exchange of spiritual knowledge. The Sierra Mazateca is a repository of profound wisdom. In such a climate, there were those who had learned to use this wisdom to help other people, and there were those who were serious negative mischief-makers.

Such is the negative connotation of the word *brujo*, meaning sorcerer or shaman. Or even more so the word *hechicero*. Words convey different things to different people. In defense of the word *brujo*, or the feminine, *bruja*, let's just say that there are some very good *brujos* and *brujas*, with great wisdom and knowledge who work for the benefit of the people, animals, plants, and elements. The excellent ones have little contact with the outside world, because they are operating on another plane of consciousness. Since in the *sierra* there is such light generated, a good amount of the dark side exists. Having witnessed numerous cases of sorcery over the years, there was no doubt that people would go to great lengths to master these dark powers. Naiveté in such a place was a serious problem. I had no point of reference.

I was learning by the Braille method. Easy-going California living had no place here. With people outside Doña Julieta's family, one had to be on guard. A more sophisticated worldview gleaned from a liberal U.C. education had no place to hang onto when confronted by the power of these ancient peoples, the Mazatecos.

One day about mid-morning, Tio Joaquin walked thorough the side entrance of the family compound. Doña Julieta and I were busy with the daily chores of caring for the children, cooking and cleaning, and tending the animals. Upon seeing him, she radiated such joy.

Tio Joaquin, her brother, exuded energy from his dapper form. Dressed simply in a freshly pressed white shirt and brown pants, his broad brimmed finely woven cream colored palm hat slightly tilted to one side, and his gold tooth cut a handsome figure, which made his smile even more inviting. His silver hair and pencil thin mustache on his clear face completed the picture.

He carried a *machete*, and a string bag, while on his worn feet were the simple sandals that most of the men wore. Elegant in his simplicity, he was equally elegant in demeanor. Quiet and soft-spoken, he was good to just be near.

Tio Joaquin was getting older and visiting less, since the journey on foot round trip took more than four hours. Visits like these were not just social. These special visits were for deeper talks between *sabios* (wise people). He walked across the patio and was offered a straight-backed simple wooden chair, in the shade out of the intense sun. After drinking a delicious cup of the coffee grown by the family, talk began as the *almuerzo*, the morning meal around eleven, was being prepared.

As story had it, Tio Joaquin was having some trouble with a *brujo* from a nearby village. At a loss for the right way to proceed, he was seeking counsel from his sister Julieta, who was a Seer. Nacho the *brujo* came from San Lucas, a village famous in the region for its sorcerers. Everyone knew that the people from that place were "*muy delicado*" (very delicate), and easily disturbed. This meant that the people of San Lucas were offended easily, so it was very important to be aware when interacting with them.

Somehow Nacho had taken offense at something Tio Joaquin did when their paths crossed. Since that time, strange and annoying things were happening at Tio Joaquin's *cabaña* (cabin), perched on the side of the mountain. Because of the remoteness, there are many strange energies in those mountains. *Brujos malos* (bad brujos) are experts at manipulating forces and spirits, which can do harm. There are *brujas malas* also.

Tio Joaquin and Doña Julieta were sitting in chairs on the outdoor patio discussing, when suddenly Tio Joaquin jumped up and shouted, running across towards the water tank. Just at that moment they saw the last half of a coral snake disappear into a hole in the wall next to the cement tank. Tio Joaquin lost no time grabbing a machete and began to dig furiously at the adobe wall. Fearless, he stuck his hand into the enlarged hole and pulled out the large coral snake.

He gave it a *machetazo*, a forceful machete slice, right there, and cut its head off. Then he skinned the snake. The meat was kept for other works, such as medicine making for serious illnesses. When Tio Joaquin saw the snake, he saw that it was the *nagual* Nacho in one of his forms. After that, Tio Joaquin found out that on the same day in San Lucas, they found the *brujo* Nacho dead. It was a case of *justicia salvaje*, savage justice.

There are many *naguals* in Mexico. These are women and men shape shifters. Taking the form of an animal, bird or reptile, *brujas* and *brujos* do magic. All over Meso-America there are many stories about shape shifters. In the Sierra Mazateca, this was part of ordinary reality.

CHAPTER 17 THE SOUND OF RUSHING WATER

The river far below the village became a refuge for me. When things got too busy at the house, I would ask permission to hike down the mountains sloping trails to the river. Through the coffee plants, through the banana trees, oaks and pines, down, down until I finally reached the rushing river. Walking along the road, which ran next to it, I headed in the direction away from the bridge, towards the waterfall.

When it was hot, this was a good place to be. Climbing down from the road among big rocks, the river was welcoming. Rushing water came down from the waterfall about thirty feet above, into the clear blue green water. This was a place that the locals came. A place of big energy.

From there I walked down the riverbank for a while until I reached my own secret spot. I had discovered this gem when I was searching for a secluded place to meditate, totally immersed in Mother Nature. It was the tree that called me. There ahead was a most magnificent tree, very old, with long sinuous roots, which stretched into the water. The great branches made a canopy to shade against the intense sun.

Beneath this great protector, the river formed a lovely bathing pool. It was just the right place to sit sky clad on the riverbank and practice meditation. The water was not too deep, and in places I could sit up to my neck with the cool water flowing by. It was a solitary place. There was no sound but the sound of rushing water.

There are certain meditations that you can do with water. These practices are dependent on place and the tone of water that the rocks make. Either in it, on it, or by it, places of water are places of spirits. These waters were fed by mountain springs. After spending who knows how long, I returned refreshed up to the family compound.

The river was known to claim a number of lives. The natives of the region were not swimmers. In some places the current was very fast. A psychologist and his wife, who I had met in Texas, requested to travel to meet Doña Julieta. I guided them to her.

They had a connection with her, and were good people, respectful and non-complaining. One day during their stay, we went down to the river to escape the heat. One of the *Nenes*, Jimmy, came with us.

We got to a place on the river where it was wider, with rocks protruding here and there. All of us were happy. Embraced by nature on a fine day, we were enraptured. Colorful butterflies in the air, birdsong, the water flowing by, the magic of the mountains was within us.

The Sierra Mazateca was famous for its caves. These caves were carved out by water through time. Some of the deepest caverns in Mexico are in this region. The rivers were directly connected with these cave systems, and there were many underground channels where the water went.

Jimmy was a daredevil. He loved the physical challenge. And so, he decided to cross the river by leaping stone to stone. In that place the river was deep enough to make one wary. He was encouraging the psychologist to follow. The last thing I saw was him starting to follow the leader. The doctor wore glasses. I noted that he did not have them on when he started to leap.

I departed from the group to go downstream to meditate, taking every opportunity to be immersed in the wilds. Finding my spot near the rivers edge, I sat peacefully for a while. Suddenly I was aroused from my equanimity by a scream coming from upriver.

I leapt up, moving towards the group, to see the doctor's wife on the riverbank watching in horror as her husband was being swept away by the swift current. She was yelling at him above the waters sound. No too far from where I was, the river went down a big hole in the earth, totally disappearing into who knows where.

The doctor was headed my way, crashing into some big boulders in the water. He was flailing in the water unable to see well. I knew that if I did not get him out somehow, he was going down the drain. I started shouting to him to swim for the shore. The urgency in my voice spiked a sprint from him, and he made it to shore, less than twenty-five yards of the last ride of his life. His wife was an emotional wreck. He sputtered up the bank, having drunk a lot of water, and collapsed.

This proved to be a big reflection for the doctor, who narrowly escaped drowning. We returned to the village after gathering ourselves from this close call. Visibly shaken, we walked into the family compound. Doña Julieta had been cooking, and noticed that the doctor and his wife had a good case of fright.

She knew exactly what to do and wasted no time. She proceeded to gather some coals from her fire and placing them into her *copalera*, and then burning *copal*, healing work was begun on both of them. Afterwards, they were visibly restored and very grateful.

Sometime later, after they had gone, Doña Julieta began giving me teachings about water. I told her that I had found a good place to meditate. She was happy for me, because she knew this was good for me. "There is one important thing that you have to know", she said. "Never go into the water when the river has her period."

"What do you mean Mamá?" Not putting together what she was saying. "In the rainy season, the river gets her period, and there are many impurities in the water. So don't go in it. Pay attention to this."

It was a warning that I would not forget. Several times after that, when I went down to the river, when the waters were running clear, I would think about what she said. I became accustomed to the subtle changes that happened in nature around my secret spot.

A few years later, after I had been away for a while, I went down to the river to check out my place. Walking on the riverbank, I spotted a glass syringe lying on the ground by the waters edge. I was horrified. This moment proved the beginning of the major changes that I was to witness in the sierra. Up to that time, plastics had not been introduced. And chemical fertilizers were just coming into the region. Environmental degradation had begun.

One day Doña Julieta told me about some doctors covering the *sierra* by foot. News between the villages travels fast. Many villagers depend on natural springs of pure water that come out of the mountains. The doctors had been going to all the springs they could find, putting chemicals in the springs in order to "purify them." This was a serious blow to the region.

The Mazatecos believe that water is sacred. Water is life. It was almost beyond thought that anyone would tamper with the water. After all, the water had its *dueño* (owner - protector) *Chicón Nandá*. It is believed that if anyone harms elements of nature, one becomes sick. These spirit illnesses manifest in many ways.

CHAPTER 18   THE MAGIC BEANS

Like a slow silent incoming fog, an inconceivable change was coming over the *sierra*. The Mazatecos were farmers, and people of the corn. Doña Julieta in her kitchen teachings one day said, "Never eat beans without a tortilla." Meaning a corn tortilla, since these people were not wheat people. Beans eaten with corn is a whole protein, and very nutritious.

The farmers in the region would grow on their traditional plots of land enough corn to feed their family, along with other greens, tomatoes, squash, beans, coffee and honey. All the seeds planted were from seeds kept for generations within the family's own seed bank. A good part of the news that reached the family compound was about agriculture. The prices of a sack of corn, or coffee, were in flux.

At an earlier point in time, the farmers were influenced to grow coffee as a cash crop to offset the usual corn cash crop. Coffee was a way of diversifying from a monoculture. Almost all of the farmers diversified in this way in hopes of getting ahead economically. The region had much poverty.

One day, Venancio returned from the *milpa* (corn field), with some disheartening news. He told us that the bottom of the coffee market had fallen out, and that the price offered for coffee was so low that it was impossible to sell the harvest for a profit. This put the household under a very tight squeeze. There was no money.

I had a long time interest in planting, and with my experience in college combined with my grandparents' teachings in their garden, and time spent on my great uncle's farm, there was something genetic within me, which needed to respond to this critical situation. The conversation soon centered on seeds. Heirloom seeds.

Venancio had been a farmer all his life, as was his father before him. All the villagers were farmers, except for the very few who decided to be merchants. The discussion centered on the economy of agriculture, and boiling it all down, the main threat was the problem of getting heirloom seed, if your own seed ran out due to crop failure. We talked about the varieties of plants under cultivation, which were all from the region, except for coffee. It was mentioned that some of the varieties of edible plants were disappearing, as well as seed stock.

At that point, I decided to begin an activity that I have been doing now for over forty years. The seed exchange. My gardening master in Santa Cruz, Ann, had a few very hardy varieties of plants, which she loyally planted annually. One of these was Scarlet Runner beans, sometimes called Roma beans. When harvest time came in her garden where I worked, I collected some of these beans.

Returning to the *sierra*, shortly after my arrival, we were sitting at the kitchen table, and I produced a bag in my hands. Holding the bag out, gifting them to Venancio, I said, "Here, these are magic beans!" Both he and Doña Julieta looked at me laughing. Fascinated by the shape and size of the bean, they showed their appreciation. They had never had seeds from the outside world. Then I went on to tell them the story of Jack and the Beanstalk and the magic beans. They liked the story, never having heard it.

In that region, as well as all over southern Mexico, the beans most eaten were black beans. They were delicious, nutritious, and hard to beat in flavor, either straight from the *olla* (the pot), or refried. Scarlet Runner beans are highly versatile, because you can eat the flower, the green bean, or the dried beans. Also the plant produces two years in a row, without the need to replant. So it is a good bean with a good yield.

The magic beans were planted on the patio so the plants' progress could be witnessed by the whole family. The children were especially interested because this bean was a great climber. This initial seed exchange was the beginning of a very big work that I was to undertake years later, through the counsel of Doña Julieta. Although I began the seed exchange with the family, the truth is that Doña Julieta was seeding me.

Little did I know that at that time I was witnessing the change of traditional indigenous agriculture, the incursion of chemical fertilizers, the poisoning of the mountain springs, the loss of heirloom seeds, and general environmental degradation. Plastics were just coming into the region. The government was pushing chemical fertilizers. The farmers, who bought into this use, were placed on a wheel of consumption, which demanded cash.

Many of the farmers who had traditionally used organic compost were opting for chemical fertilizers, which promised higher yields at harvest. A split in thinking was taking place. Farmers were going into debt for the fertilizers. When the price of coffee crashed, fertilizer loans could not be repaid. A very big problem developed in the region, causing desperation.

I was seeing what hunger looked like. Silent and deadly. The desperation manifested itself in over consumption of alcohol to ease the pain, this provoked social problems to surface. A chain of events, which would take place many times over in agricultural communities on different places of the planet.

Good harvest meant a flowing economy. When the economy was so tight, all eyes were on the local politicians to set things straight. In the regional capitol of Huautla, emotions ran high amongst the politically minded. Violence was not uncommon between opposing political party members.

As this political intrigue was going on, the Mazatec elders continued their task of holding ceremonies on the sacred spots in the mountains to insure that the *dueños* (the owners- the spirits in charge) were paid in beauty. These *pagos* (payments) were like a spiritual insurance policy for the well being of all the people.

Oaxaca was one of the poorest states in Mexico. Poor in money, and rich in culture and heirloom seeds. It was a place that the much larger forces were eyeing for exploitation. Of note, historically, when Cortés chose which region he wanted out of all the land in Mexico as a land grant from the King of Spain, he chose Oaxaca. And unknown to him that Oaxaca contained one of the greatest spiritual treasures of the planet.

There was a new conflict brewing. It was a conflict of values, of orientation, of the continuation of life as it had been known since ancient times. This conflict centered around agriculture and the way it was done. Ultimately it centered on the holy heirloom corn seed. No one could possibly imagine the impact of biotechnology creating genetically modified organisms (GMO), being introduced into the food chain.

What lab tech at Monsanto in Missouri or U.C. Davis doing gene splicing on corn and other organisms could possibly understand about the connections of their actions and the disastrous implications to indigenous culture and life itself on our holy Earth Mother?

Pandora's box had been opened. I was to see some of the truly horrifying results. Hormone disruption in the youth who consumed these GMO's unknowingly, skin allergies, and food allergies in the general populace were rampant. In Latin America, the massive consumption of sodas, sweetened with GMO corn syrup, along with daily GMO yellow corn intake seemed to be a disastrous combination. Ann's magic beans, combined with Doña Julieta's visionary insight would guide me into being a seed warrior.

Doña Julieta Pineda Pereda

"I was born there, Huatla de Jiménez."

Sacred mushrooms of the Sierra Mazatec

Derrumbes (landslides) Psilocybe caerulescens

Coatlicue – Lady of the Serpent Skirts
An artist's visionary form of the Mother Goddess with sacred mushrooms and cosmic symbology. Tehuacán, Puebla mural.

Dr. Richard Evans Schultes and pre-Columbian artifacts collection in the Wasson library, Harvard University.

CHAPTER 19   CROSSING PATHS WITH THE GUIDE

It is one thing to go on look about, walk about or drive about in search of a teacher, a guide, who can surely put you on the path. It is another thing to actually find a guide, and not only any guide but an authentic living master. People have ideas of how a master should look or behave. Many authentic masters are totally unconventional.

   Coming from my American culture into an indigenous culture was like leaping realities. My education in school was dominated by the patriarchy, which also dominated language, books written and studied skewing ancient knowledge handed down. The majority of teachers in my university education were men.

   Fortunately, I came from a family where the matriarchy ruled. I searched with great thirst to learn and study among scholars and gurus, in many lands. After it all, to my amazement, I crossed paths with an authentic guide and she was a woman. She was married with a family, and was a healer.

   On contemplating this, what incredible fortune I had to not only meet her, but also to apprentice with and be adopted by her. What were the chances that I travel to such a distant place to cross paths with her? What were the connectors? And most of all what kept me coming back…

   Something so simple, and so missing in my life was that opportunity to receive the teachings from Doña Julieta. And not only from her, but also from the plants that she was the emissary for. The deep connectedness, the energetic glue that I was seeking was in the power plants.

During my undergrad years at UCSC, it happened to be the time of what I call the First Turning of the Psychedelic Wheel of the Dharma. We were traveling in Leary's tail wind. Everyone was reading Castaneda, and we all wanted to know what was with these plant teachers. Up at the City on a Hill as the University is called there, almost everyone was tripping on something sometime. The campus area was ideal because it was located in a removed place from the town surrounded by redwood forest. Big yellow banana slugs, which abounded there, took on a new meaning when your senses were heightened through the plant teachers.

Getting altered was part of the program. Yet to what end? Trying to get there through other methods was the reason I started to study Yoga. At that time, very few people were interested in discipline. I was schooled in a highly disciplined way, and so it was not difficult for me.

My desire to learn led me to be with an authentic yoga master from India, who I studied with for a few years. He carefully guided me in my studies of Ayurveda. During the time I apprenticed with Doña Julieta, I had the chance to do graduate work. I lived in India, and studied with the Ayurvedic greats at the time, at Benares Hindu University. It was a tremendous privilege.

There is much more to the India story, however, let it suffice to say that it was highly refreshing to meet and study with an authentic indigenous woman master from the land of my ancestors. Doña Julieta was humble and full of grace. It was rare to see her lose her cool. She was as tough as she was beautiful.

With me, she always was kind, and when I would arrive

unannounced, since in those days there was no telephone in the village, I was always received with open arms. This was the life in the village. People just showed up. And when people showed up, whether friend or patient, sometimes, the family would put you up. Sometimes for a day, sometimes for a week or longer. This is the way it was. Whatever there was was shared.

Among native people, the main word that rules all activities with others is *confianza* (trust). This was a big lesson for me. In the world that I came from, I was an innocent, trusting all. During my time with Doña Julieta, I learned through experience the value of trust in others. I learned to watch behavior, and motivation.

When you are in a distant land, you have to have your antennas out as to whom you can trust. Once when traveling alone up into the *sierra*, I was waiting for a bus around 3 a.m. under a street light, with a few other natives. It was so unusual for them to see a lone woman from the outside world. A drunk came near me and decided to speak to me and get close. I was sitting down with my pack, just waiting and good naturedly putting up with this guy. After awhile, he began to lay his head on my shoulder to doze off. This was too much! Up I stood and then saw a cargo truck with the name of Doña Julieta's village on it.

I knew the driver was headed up to the village, about four hours away, and so I went up to ask for a ride. He had another woman in the cab with him, and told her to move over to the window so I could sit next to him. This was the first sign that in my innocence, I missed. He had two guys who were his assistants, traveling in the back of the big truck.

The bus up into the mountains was delayed from its 4 a.m. departure. So I was happy thinking that I would arrive in the village in good time traveling by truck. The ride seemed like a boon at the time. So we took off up the mountain. There was a lot of talk, during which the driver told me that he was not going up to the village directly. He said he was taking cargo to another village some distance in another direction from where I was going. I started to get a bad feeling.

The road was in disrepair as usual, and it was slow going in this lumbering beast. Finally we made it to the Plan de Guadalupe, where we stopped. We were told to stay in the truck. The driver got down, and after a few minutes had a group of men around the front of the truck. He was pointing to me and speaking in Mazateco. Somehow, I knew what he was saying. I knew that I was in real danger. Day was just beginning to break. The men were all looking at me and laughing. Then something diverted their attention and they walked away from the truck.

Suddenly I realized this was my chance to make a break for it. I felt something lifting me up out of the seat, as if not by my own doing. I jumped out of the truck. One of the guys was in the back, and I told him to throw down my pack and extra bag of gifts. He looked at me quizzically but obeyed my order. I grabbed my things, and just then heard the bus coming.

It stopped nearby, and I made way for the door loaded down with my stuff. As I tried to get up onto the first step, the weight of my pack pulled me backwards. I felt invisible hands pushing me from behind. Just then, two young native guys came forward and held out their hands to help me on. This was very unusual.

Thanking them, I swung around to sit in the first seat by the window. I thought that these young men must be angels. The bus driver delayed a few minutes before leaving. In the wait, the driver of the cargo truck discovered that I had left, foiling his plan. He was so irate. I could see him fuming.

He sent his assistant to the bus to tell me to get off and get back in the truck! I told him no emphatically. Then he began to harass me insisting that I pay the driver for the ride! He was so nasty that he caused everyone on the bus to wonder what was going on. The bus driver being savvy, started to pull away. I threw some money out the window, with the guy outside still yelling. WHEW!

Settling into the rest of the journey, I traveled on several hours to where I had to get off at the *puente* (bridge). It was very early morning as I stepped down from that old school bus which was the only public transport. I waved to my angels before they proceeded up to Huautla, and thanked the driver.

There I was, with two heavy bags, and a one hour climb before me. Lucky for me there were two young men who had gotten off the bus at the same time, also going up to the village. After some talk, telling them who I was going to see, I asked for some help carrying. One of the young men smiled knowingly and volunteered to carry the heaviest bag. I carried the other and off we went. It was a hard climb. I was panting on the trail, not having eaten or drunk anything for hours.

Because of the weight of my bag, it took much longer to cover the distance. Finally entering the edge of the village down the way from the house, they left me to carry the rest alone. I struggled with the weight, and made it to the worn wooden gate.

Knocking loudly, finally someone came to the door. It was Chavela. Smiling, she helped me in, and took me into the kitchen to sit. Doña Julieta had not yet come downstairs. Chavela went to get her. When she came, just seeing her made me burst out in tears.

Chavela ran to make coffee. Doña Julieta held me and let me cry releasing the energy. I was so happy to have made it.

She calmed me down, and after some coffee, I began to recount the tale of my adventure to get there. I told her about the truck and the driver. As I was telling her, she sucked in her breath. She looked at me and said, "We know who this is. He would have killed you."

CHAPTER 20 TRUSTING THE JOURNEY

Once you have met an authentic guide, it is necessary to totally give yourself over to the journey. Sometimes you make a plan, and suddenly it all dissolves. Any kind of rigid thinking has to be thrown out the window. You have to learn to shift gears quickly. Zig instead of zag.

I had made plans to return to see Doña Julieta and her family for Christmas. Arriving in Mexico City, I connected with Hippie, who was grown now. The initial plan was to travel with him up to the village, supposedly leaving on the late night bus.

My concept was that we were to travel in the direction of the Sierra Mazateca. I was told that we were to get on a bus to connect with her in Oaxaca, south. Oaxaca? Major change of plan from my idea of spending a peaceful holiday up in the village.

What I was in for was totally unexpected, and a real test. Hippie explained to me that the whole family was gathering outside of Oaxaca City, to celebrate the baptism of the first grandson. We traveled many hours and arrived to a city in celebration. Very tired, we got a hotel, and spent the night.

One of the most beautiful places at Christmas time is Oaxaca. The weather is excellent, and there are many unusual things to see like the *Noche de Rabanos* (the Night of the Radishes). This is a contest to see who could make the most clever carvings out of the radishes. There are many sizes of radishes grown there and the art made of radishes was astounding. Many people came in from the country to see this, as well as international visitors in the know.

After some rest, we communicated with one of the brothers, who told us to come to the eldest brothers house in a village some half an hour outside of the city. So off we went by taxi. We arrived to a big family scene. The small house could hardly contain all the family members. There were a lot of kids running around. Doña Julieta and the family were glad I made it for the *fiesta* (party). She was in good spirits since she had just arrived from a pilgrimage to the Virgin of Juquila.

It was Christmas Eve, and the way that it was celebrated was far different than I had ever experienced. Some of the family members had traveled a long way to get there, and had not seen the rest of the family for a long time. So it was a big reunion centering around the baptism of little Gerardo.

I was still tired from the journey, so all the commotion was a lot for me to handle. I thought that I would stay for a few hours and then make it back to my hotel in the city because there was no place to sleep in the house. It was bulging at the seams with the family.

Doña Julieta, being the grand matriarch, was directing the show. The siblings pooled funds and bought a lot of food. Appetizers were going around and there were drinks flowing. The evening started to progress, and I began to fade. I asked the brothers to find me a cab.

After waiting awhile, they said that there was no transport to be had back to the city. So I had to acquiesce, and take it all in. So many stories, so much music, so much food and so much drink. Everyone was in a festive mood. Time flowed on as it neared midnight.

I thought that by now people would like to go to sleep, but no!

Just when I was starting to get a grip of what was actually happening, just nearing twelve, out walked Doña Julieta onto the patio with a bunch of meat ready for cooking. She had started a midnight barbecue for the entire family of almost twenty people!!! Unbelievable!

Firecrackers started going off in the village at midnight, and people were out in the streets celebrating. On the patio of the house everyone was gathered, joyfully, sharing toasts. It seemed like everyone had gotten their second wind and were up for the next round.

There she was, the big Mama, cooking for everyone at midnight. There was a lot of noise from the fireworks and celebration. All the kids were running around, and a piñata (made of colorful paper mache in the form of animals usually, around a clay pot, or a hollow place within to hold candies, nuts, and sometimes money) was produced for the enjoyment of all.

Everyone got blindfolded and took a turn at trying to break the *piñata*, suspended by a rope thrown over a high tree branch. There was a lot of merriment. When the piñata got bashed enough with the stick, the contents poured out, delighting the children who scrambled to pick up the contents.

Doña Julieta finished cooking on the grill, and everyone ate a huge meal. When I was done eating, she came over to me. She held my arm and took me to a quiet corner and pointed to the stars blazing in the clear night sky. She started to explain about the stars and their names in Mazateco. She had a far away look in her eyes, like she was in ecstasy. She held me close. It was in that state that we stayed for a little while before our reverie was broken by one of the family members.

Whisked away, she went on to share with the other children. Everyone was absolutely content. The party continued on with music and dancing. As time moved on, my battery was running low and I really wanted to leave. Once again mentioning this to the eldest brother, I was told that there were no taxis to be had for at least a few more hours. And so, I had to wait. They would not let me go out onto the street alone.

I was totally unprepared for that level of fiesta. This was my learning curve, because when they throw a fiesta in Oaxaca like this, it lasts until dawn. By nature, I am not one for much fiesta, but now was my turn to get into another way of being. All the family members were talking and joking, drinking and dancing. It was lively.

By the time 4 a.m. came, I was fried. I could not eat or drink another thing. I was done. I wanted to leave very badly, and just go to sleep. Finally, after another little while, transport was located and off I went, bidding the family goodbye until the next day.

I arrived at my hotel just after dawn on Christmas morning. I fell into the bed and had a deep sleep. Before mid-day, the youngest brother came for me. We went onto the street to enjoy the festivities at the *zócalo* (central plaza). There was so much color, music and many people. It was joyous.

We returned to the eldest brothers house a little later, where the *fiesta* had resumed after everyone had a few hours sleep. Once again embraced by the family, the food and drink flowed again. There was much story and catching up to do among the brothers and sisters. Some hours passed, and then I was invited to travel with Doña Julieta and some of the family members to visit a master potter in another village in the vicinity famous for its black pottery.

When we arrived, we parked and walked into his showroom. He

was very surprised and absolutely delighted to see Doña Julieta. She had healed him of an infirmity and he was beside himself in gratitude. While they talked, I wandered around, looking at his most beautiful creations. He made very big pots, some three to four feet tall, all beautifully burnished.

After awhile, we left, everyone happy. The sun was hot as I rode in the back of the open truck with some kids. Ah Oaxaca! We made it back to the house, and I decided to take my space returning to my hotel. They partied on.

Doña Julieta told me to meet them the next morning at the church for the baptism. So, at the appointed time, I showed up, staying in the back of the crowd in the church. After the brief ceremony, I discovered I was in for another round of *fiesta*!!!

Off we went en masse to a private place they had rented to hold the *fiesta*. We arrived at the place to be ushered under a big white canopy, almost like a circus tent. There, even more of the extended family showed up for the big fling.

Once again after a little while, I had had enough. So I told Doña Julieta that I was going to leave and she told the boys to get me a cab. I said I would take the bus, since the place was near the highway leading to the city. They would not hear of it and insisted that I stay until transport could be found.

I had begun to lose patience because many of the men were very spaced out on *aguardiente*. Truthfully, I was totally *fiesta'd* out. Finally the transport came through after dark, and I made it back to my room. There I gave thanks for arriving safely and having made it through the last few days.

The next morning early, the family picked me up and I was sent into the market to buy fresh meat that we would carry home. Other items purchased were sweet bread, and vegetables, to have ample supply for everyone through the New Year. It was a Christmas I would never forget.

CHAPTER 21   THE LITTLE WHITE SHOES

It was a long journey riding in the back of that cargo truck all the way into the mountains. I had been given the luxury seat, on top of two mattresses, enclosed by boxes against the wind. Blue sky above and perfect weather, it was a great ride. The only difficulty was the fuel in the big drum that sometimes leaked when we hit a bump. I was glad I wasn't asphyxiated. Late afternoon found us in Teotitlán del Camino, waiting to gas up in a long line of vehicles at the last gas station before climbing the sierra.

I stood up in the back of the cargo truck looking out, and saw a big storm coming our way in the distance. Big dark billowing clouds. Other people in the line noticed it also. I tapped on top of the cab and told the family inside. While we waited for gas, we all put a big tarp well tied down on the back of the truck covering everything. There was just enough room for me to look out from the back. Night started to fall as we began our climb up the mountain. I noticed the wind was picking up. We traveled on for a while.

All of a sudden the truck came to a stop. That was the first obstacle. Paco tried to start the truck again but it wouldn't turn over and then finally he jumped out of the truck and asked me to throw him his raincoat, which was in the back. I found out that he didn't have a flashlight. In that instant I realized what my intuition had been telling me before I left for Mexico. Take extra flashlights.

Here we were out in the middle of the Sierra Mazateca, stuck in total darkness and pouring rain. Thank goodness I had brought along a number of disposable flashlights. Before the journey would be over we would have finished all of them but one. I fished around among all the bags that we were carrying, Braille method, in total blackness, and located my flashlight stash. I gave Paco one. He looked into the gas tank and then we tried to siphon gas from the gasoline drum lashed in the back, with not much success initially. The rain was coming down in torrents. Who knows what the real problem was.

Paco being a mechanic made me feel a little better about the situation. But the gasoline just wouldn't enter into the tank. There must have been something wrong with the line. He told me that the gas tank in the truck was empty.

Finally, the gas started to enter the gas tank. Paco worked very hard at it. Then, after putting the rest of the gear back into the truck, we left, roaring up into the mountains. Relieved, and ecstatic to be moving again, I stuck my head out of the back end of the overhead tarp and let out a mighty YEE HA as we took off. The power of the yell was absorbed in the blowing wind and pelting rain in the inky blackness.

It was one of those nights neither fit for man nor beast. It was pouring down in a torment of rain and quite cold. The clouds were closing in over the road and even though the road had been paved, in this kind of weather on those kind of tortuous curves, it was quite dangerous. We traveled a long way on the paved road and finally after great length, I could feel the truck slow down to the point where we got off the paved road. This was the turning off point near the swollen river, where we started to go up towards the village. I had heard before we left Oaxaca, having received word from our household in the mountains that the road up into the village was completely closed off due to rain and mud.

There had been an alternative plan put forth that we would take a back road into the village. The route would be even more winding and long from the Plan de Guadalupe. Actually I had thought that Paco was taking that route but when we started to go off of the paved road I realized that we had taken the normal route and I wondered what lay before us. The rain had started to let up by that time but the mud was deep in places and very slick. I didn't know exactly what time it was, but it was quite late at night. We had already been on the road for at least ten hours.

Once we passed the flat part by the river and started to climb, on the very first curve, we started to hit real trouble. All of a sudden I felt the truck start to slide sideways. I got this peculiar feeling in my stomach I have had many times before coming up into these mountains. It was that feeling of serious danger.

I had remembered that every time coming up into the mountains in the rain had always been a pilgrimage. Of course now the roads had changed so much and were so much improved, it was nothing like the past. Not long before, for years we braved serious danger traveling on single lane muddy tracks in the dead of night to get there. What I always remembered was that Mother Nature was so strong in those mountains, that no man or machine could ever conquer her.

As the truck slid sideways, it came to a halt. I heard Paco and Venancio get out and check out the situation. Then I heard Julieta get out. She had been wearing her very best dress that she had worn to the baptism of her grandson the day before down in Oaxaca, with her tiny, white, high heels. A slight argument broke out as to what to do.

I peeked my head out of the back of the truck to survey the situation. On an incline, the truck had slid in the mud and was right at the edge of the road. At the very edge of the road had been piled a bunch of rocks, and from there, the slope went down. Way down. For months, roadwork was being done on that road, bulldozers pushing through up to the village, to straighten and flatten the once burro trail, so eventually the pavers could come and put down asphalt. But as work goes in the mountains, you never know when things will be completed, and sure enough, with the road being cut by the dozers and no rock being put down on it, when the rains came, the road became a serious obstacle for wheeled travel.

There was a lot of discussion as to what to do. The little disposable flashlights gave out little light to see what was going on. To say the least the situation was precarious. We were within two feet from going off the edge of the road. I climbed down off the truck, and all of us were walking around in the mud, trying to figure out how to get out of the situation we were in. I checked my watch, it was midnight, pitch black, out in the mountains, and I thought to myself, so near and yet so far from the village.

We were a good thirty minutes away, and I started to imagine what it would take to get up to the village from there. And then I started thinking what would happen to all of the luggage that was so heavy in the back of the truck, especially my bags, which were filled with supplies, and gifts that I had brought from the States.

I shifted my attention and energy to Doña Julieta, who walked around the truck, and began to do her magic. She had taken out her San Pedro, a protection medicine, and cast it around the truck and began praying loudly in Mazateco. It was really a sight to see her by the beam of the truck lights, encased in fog in the slight distance, with the only thing visible, those tiny white high heels on seemingly disembodied feet walking in the deep mud, throwing her medicine.

Venancio and Paco were trying to decide which would be the best way to try to get the truck out of its predicament. I checked it out myself and decided to throw in my two cents, having driven up into those mountains for years before and being in similar situations. It was a really hard thing to look at, knowing that one false move, and that would be it for the truck. Tow trucks aren't too handy in those places. One mistake and not only is your truck finished for a long time but also it costs you a bundle to get out of your mistake.

So I talked to Paco and gave him my ideas about how he should do it to try to get the truck down the hill in one piece. It was very edgy and the situation was very, very intense. Finally we were all in accord as to what to do and I told Paco we had to come down inch by inch because any kind of velocity would just cause the truck to slide even more. It would be completely out of control as the mud had built up on the tires. There was absolutely no traction to be had, even though we were only on a slight grade.

Finally it was decided that Paco would try to back it up a little bit and we were going to push on the right side. I couldn't believe within myself that this was going to work at all because we were like little ants in comparison to that mountain of a truck. However, we all went for it as he started to let off the brake. And for some ungodly reason our slight weight against the back of the truck was enough to get it straightened out. Sliding as it was, we countered the major bulk of the truck and we were able to slowly, slowly roll it back down the hill. We were pushing against the truck and praying.

I noticed the headlights of two pickup trucks that had stopped at the bottom of the hill. Those people had been traveling from the city of Tehuacán to come back up into the mountains. It was a miracle to me that there were people on that road at that hour, behind us. As things happen for me, the angels appeared just when I needed them, and this, for sure, was one of those cases. Both of those pickups had come from our village and had gone out to do business and were returning at a late hour.

Miraculously we got the truck backed up all the way to a flat part on the hill. The other people in the pickup trucks offered us a ride up to the village even though one of the trucks was literally piled with merchandise that they had bought in the city to bring back. Somehow we managed to put all of my bags and the foodstuffs into the back of the pickup truck. Doña Julieta rode in front. The rest of us piled in the back, amongst several other men, local villagers who were riding in the back. And then, we took off to go up the mountain.

We caravanned with the other truck behind us. It was slip and slide all the way up. Things were piled all around us, the truck lurched forward, things were falling, and I was grabbing onto anything I could. All of us were tense in the back knowing that the truck could just stop anytime due to the mud.

The truck was totally packed, maybe even overloaded. I was sitting on top of some crates of chickens. Suddenly the truck started to fishtail in the mud. Spontaneously out of my mouth came loud prayers asking for all obstacles to be removed. All the men looked at me, incredulous. I kept praying, only wanting to arrive safely. The bumpy ascent seemed to take forever.

Suddenly, we were there, delivered safely to the door of Doña Julieta and Venancio's house. When the gear was unloaded, and the pickup drove away, the front door flung open. There in the dim light, in front of us, was a Christmas manger scene, with a life size statue of the baby Jesus. Doña Julieta stepped in and fell to her knees, adoring the Christ child in gratitude for our safe arrival.

CHAPTER 22   OUT OF MY COMFORT ZONE

Doña Julieta started teaching me about medicinal plants from her own garden. There were many varieties of plants that I had never seen before. She had an upper garden in her patio, and then another small plot on the lower level of the house.

She was a master herbalist, and in her plots were a variety of psychotropic plants. The mountains were a veritable living pharmacy. I had begun to be taught medicinal plants when I was a child by my grandmother, and later in California. Some of my earliest memories were being sent out to the garden to pick plants. I learned herbs and vegetables. Later I learned about the different kinds of fruits in the garden. My grandmother was especially fond of her flowers, and May was the month of many sweet smelling flowers, which I picked many of. Within my own family, we were plant people.

Along with the medicinal plants in Doña Julieta's garden were herbs used in the kitchen. Flowers were planted among the green plants. Starting with the culinary herbs, I began asking questions about their properties.

She had me tasting many plants, and explained their uses. Doña Julieta opened up and continuously taught me. One plant in particular caught my attention. Its stalk was square. This was one of the ally plants to the sacred mushrooms, skaa pastora (the leaves of the shepherdess).

In order to properly apprentice with the power plants, you have to go through a number of cleanses. One of the first that I had to endure was the *purga* (purge). One day, Doña Julieta had determined that it was my time to begin to cleanse. She gathered some green leaves and ground them on the *metate* and then mixing the green pulp with spring water into a glass, called me to come and drink.

I downed the green stuff as quick as I could. I had no reference point for my mind to work with in anticipation of the effects, when suddenly the body took over. Massive waves of contractions hit my innards. The outhouse one story below, down the steps, was too far to go. The drink provoked huge nausea, and at the same time a rush of diarrhea hit.

The body bolted for the door leading to the mule shed, and along side it's wooden walls, as fast as I could, dropped my drawers. I felt like I was exploding. Hit by waves of uncontrollable intensity, there I was grabbing onto a tree to steady myself from toppling over. Its shade my only comfort from the intense sun.

When my lower realm desisted the upper tract heaved. Again and again, until I felt that I was being purged on all levels. My mind felt purged, like something big was leaving with every heave. The leaves made me swoon and lose balance. I was glad the tree was there. More and more came out until I was really wasted. I could hardly take care of myself.

Doña Julieta came out to check on my progress. "*Ay Mamá!!! Que me diste?*" (Oh Mama, what did you give me?) She looked at me, and then began to study the ground, where the green remains of my lower tract lie. "*Umm, bien, muy bien!*" (Oh, good, very good!), she said. I was still reeling.

She helped me up. I was a mess. She got me to some water to

clean up. Then she made me some healing herb tea. I slowly began to recuperate. This was the beginning of many close encounters with the plants. "And this was only half the dose," she said, smiling mischievously.

La purga is an integral part of traditional native medicine. Emetics of a wide variety have historically been used by indigenous people to alleviate many illnesses. My introduction to this process was begun a few years before arriving in the *sierra* through practicing pancha karma (the five yogic cleanses). These are five yoga purification practices used for physical cleansing, some which use salt water producing vomiting. Through practice over time, I learned to vomit well.

As is custom in many of the indigenous homes in Meso-America, Doña Julieta had a sweat lodge, a *temazcal*. The *temazcal* is used for cleansing and healing, through wet steam and herbs, prayer and song. Used since pre-Columbian times, it was an integral part of native spirituality. When Cortés came to Mexico, he outlawed *temazcals*, on pain of death. His priests thought these were places where the natives conversed with the devil. The *temazcal* became an object of repression. It also became a symbol of resistance. I had done native sweat lodges in the north, and I wanted to be in a *temazcal*.

The *temazcal* was on the lower level of the house. It was a more private area, where you could not be seen. My time came one afternoon when Doña Julieta told me that we were going to have a *temazcal*. At the appointed time we walked down the stairs, passed the outhouse, past the turkey, and not far from the *cuchi* (the pig). There in front of me was a small rectangular hut, about waist high, made of stone and mud, with a low doorway covered by a blanket, and on one end a fire, built outside against the far stone wall, burning down to coals. The fire was tended by Chavelita, the *anciana* (ancient one or old one).

We quickly undressed, and Chavelita held up the entrance covering. Doña Julieta went in first. I crawled in after her, and she said, "Lay down next to me on the *petate* (woven palm mat)." With our heads pointed away from the firewall, the inside of the *temazcal* just accommodated our small bodies.

Chavelita kneeled down crouched in the doorway, with the blanket over her back, letting in just enough light to barely see her as she began to doctor us. It was already pretty hot inside the tight enclosed space. Darkness engulfed us. Then she began to pour.

In a small clay pot of water in front of her on the bare earth, floated a *jicara* (a gourd), the cantaloupe sized ones that grow at the coast, cut in half and dried. We were silent and lay still. Slowly without a word she began to pour water with the *jicara* onto the stones on the wall at our feet.

An instant blast of steam came over us. Then the next gourd full hit the stones, making them sizzle. The only sound was the hiss of the stones. It was very intense. I had my eyes closed, and then when I opened them and saw Chavelita bent over in the doorway, covered over by the blanket, half in and half out of the *temazcal*, I could not believe how she could handle the heat. She seemed indestructible.

After another gourd poured, and the steam so intense, Doña Julieta told me to turn over. We rolled in unison, now on our stomachs. Without a word, suddenly I felt the sharp lash of leafy branches across my back and down the length of my body. Each lash made my body recoil tensing up, and then with the heat, it relaxed back down.

Doña Julieta received the same lashing as I did. We received this plant medicine several times over, and then more steam enveloped our bodies. We were sweating pretty good by then. Chavelita said something in Mazateco. "What did she say?" I asked. Doña Julieta's response was, "She wanted to know if you were still alive."

After a few more pourings, the rocks started to cool. We turned over, and the blanket was lifted over the door, and we crawled out. Pretty wasted, I was received by one of the kids, who held up a sheet to wrap me in not letting the air penetrate. I was taken to a bed and tightly wrapped head to toe in the sheet topped off with a blanket.

For me this was the real capper. The Mazatecos use what I dubbed the double cooked method of sweating. The *temazcal* extended to the afterwards when you got cooked again in the sheets. I was not ready for this.

The intensity of the inside of the *temazcal* had stretched me. But this, this! I lay there being told to not uncover until I cooled down. I could hardly move, and I felt like I was in a pressure cooker. When it was impossible to endure, feeling like I was going to explode, I struggled to free my hands, head and feet, to let some cool air hit my body. The sheet was wrapped so tight, that I had to wrestle to get free. Once unbound, I immediately headed for the water tank, where I jumped in the lower bathing area and got under running water.

Over time it became harder to get wood to fire the *temazcal*. The mountains were slowly under assault. Wood is one of the basic necessities for people who live in the country. The usual sight of farmers returning from their fields with their burros or mules laden with firewood was changing. The trees, the water, and the harvests were the signs telling this story.

CHAPTER 23   THE MEDICINE WAY

In the study of plants for healing, all plants are considered medicines. Some of the actions of plants can be learned from books. In traditional native medicine or *curanderismo* (healing medicine), there are many kinds of plants, fungi, cacti, minerals, reptiles, animals and insects used.

Learning plants from a *curandera* (healer) was a lengthy process and one learned by experience. For me the emetics (*purga*) were very difficult. The various therapies, including *temazcal*, *limpias* (cleanses), massage, purgatives, herbs, reading weather, divination, the use of animals, ridding of spirits, extractions, counseling, and soul retrieval were administered according to each patient's need.

Being in Doña Julieta's household over time allowed me to see how traditional native medicine was lived. Patients with all kinds of complaints came, some from great distances by foot or on horseback. Being a traditional native doctor, a *curandera*, was no easy job. She was a servant to the community and a midwife.

What was so remarkable about Doña Julieta was her energy. She was truly amazing accomplishing so much for so many, doing healings, cooking and taking care of her family. Many times her day started before daybreak, and when ceremonies were done, she was up until very late.

The Medicine Way that Doña Julieta practiced was focused on the sacred mushrooms. In our many discussions about this wondrous medicine, she would tell me, "It is a panacea." She explained to me that from ancient times, the people in that region used the sacred mushrooms for healing. When there were no other medicines available, the sacred mushrooms would be used.

The ritualistic use of power plants to heal people has been advocated by shamans, better known in the region as *sabios* (wisdom holders), *curanderas* or *curanderos*, for millennia in many cultures on earth. The purpose of the use of power plants is to open energy blockages within the body and mind. However, the main purpose for the employment of power plants by shamans or patients is to enhance a spiritual awakening through revelation that many times takes the form of catharsis, provoking a complete breakthrough and deep healing. This is achieved through the sacred medicine and ritual done by the shaman.

The power plants are all psychotropic plants, and some entheogenic. The latter meaning those which allow direct access to the divine. Within this realm, other sacred plants are in the cacti and fungal forms. They grow in mountains, deserts and jungles. Many parts of these precious plants are used, from the roots to the seeds. Various species are used from different climatic conditions, and they are collected according to season, time of day, and phase of the moon. In certain regions, only virgin girls collect these plants.

Keepers of these spiritual sacred plant traditions have been arduously trained in their use to treat people suffering from serious mental, physical and spiritual illnesses. This training entails long-term use of the power plants under the supervision of a shaman who is a master of propitiation, manipulation and control of energetic forces, spirits, and psychic phenomena. The *sabio(a)* is the interface between the supernatural and the mundane.

The apprentice must learn how to use the medicines, attend the *curandero(a)*, and the patient during the ceremonies. Endurance is essential. Lengthy practices of physical austerities, mental and spiritual disciplines were required. No complaining. The apprentice sometimes is required to ingest the power plants with the patient to aid the *curandero(a)* in diagnosis or to be a channel for treatment. Also the apprentice has to gather the materials used for ritual, and learn the building of altars, songs, chants, and *pasos* (energetic movements).

There are three main varieties of sacred mushrooms used in the region. *Pajaritos* (Little Birds), *San Isidro* (Saint Isidore), and *derrumbes* (landslides) are the names that they are known by. They were also called *payasos* (clowns) or *niños* (children). Sometimes they were called Niños Santos (holy children). Highly prized and unusual to see were the *camotes* (sclerotia - small root like sections). In general all were known as *hongos* (mushrooms).

The Mazatecos are a culture that to this day follows the Medicine Way of the sacred mushrooms. The Sierra Mazateca still maintains a culture of *sabios*, manifested in *curanderismo* with this sacred knowledge intact. These entheogenic fungi are spoken of in hushed reverence among the indigenous people.

Traditionally, the healings done with the sacred mushrooms were done in a ceremony called a *velada*. Ceremony was the key. At the time of the ceremony, held at night when the calm of darkness aided the recipients, the mushroom doctor would do a divination. This done in the beginning gave an indication as to how many mushrooms were to be eaten. The sacred mushrooms were always eaten whole and in pairs.

Ceremony performed by a trained guide was essential. Usually the mushroom doctor received transmission in a family lineage. One was either born into the family or adopted. The secrets of the medicine, and therapies were strictly guarded.

Preparation was needed before the ceremony, and these preliminaries, as well as what the patient needed to do after the ceremony were important to the healing process. These details are what the guide helps the patient with. Some of the preparations before ceremony include fasting, special diet and purging the body. Depending on the illness to be cured, certain numbers of medicine ceremonies are done. The more difficult the illness, the more ceremony is needed. After the ceremony, one day of total rest, without much talk, and no travel, so that the body energies can reintegrate and balance, is indicated.

There is purification with copal smoke and a blessing given during the ceremony. Medicine songs and chanting are done. When the spirits start to work, many times the totally unexpected happens. After seeing truly hair raising healing experiences with spirit possessions, I knew deeply that anyone doing this medicine without a trained guide was totally crazy. When you eat the medicine, you become very open to all kinds of unknown energies. Always, the ceremony ended with an act of gratitude.

Getting this kind of education made me think of my undergrad years of experimentation with mind medicines. We had access to it all at UCSC. I knew of a few LSD psychedelic casualties who did not recover. The sacred mushrooms are nothing to mess with. Why? Because the Great Mother will kick your ass.

Sitting for many people in ceremony, I have seen unimaginable scenes manifest in people when they are purged. The sacred mushrooms are profound. It is because of their spiritual power that they are feared and outlawed in many places. The Catholic priests traveling with the conquistadores in Mexico outlawed the sacred mushrooms on pain of death. The Conquest had demonized that which is holy. Of course, they never ate the sacred flesh. The same level of mentality prevails today within the law of many countries.

    The path of healing with power plants is a secret and sacred way, preserved by few for the benefit of many. It is a holy way, a steep path, a beauty way. It is a path of tremendous joy, especially when a shaman witnesses an incredible healing. In those moments, when the sacred is palpable, the *sabia* shares in the ecstatic praise of the divine, with a deep realization that all of the effort in their hard won preparation was just for that moment. Within the great sisterhood and brotherhood of the sacred medicines, unalterable adoration and love for the creative intelligence of the universe of universes, and our holy Mother Earth, reigns indelibly impressed on our spirits, as our gift.

CHAPTER 24 FLIGHT OF THE SHAMANESS

I am liberated from this Earth. Form dissolves and all that there is, is perception. Perception without thought. Exquisitely colored light forms and patterns appear and I allow the growing energy within to move by breathing and relaxing. I let go.

It is a dazzling sight and thoroughly enchanting. The mushroom beings make themselves known to me, surround me and joyfully say, "Welcome, welcome! We are so glad that you have come!" These are the spirits of the mushrooms. I feel deeply loved and well received. They then usher my spirit deeper, deeper, into other dimensions.

I see with my disembodied eye, and hear with disembodied ear. I am taken to see an ancient native culture; they look like Mexicas, with many colored feathered headdresses. I hear their exquisite pre-Columbian music, drums, flutes and conch shell horns. I feel the deep spirituality of this ancient race and feel their cosmic origins. Somehow I feel a part of this, a connectedness, and knowingness.

I get the deep impression, as if something is indelibly stamped into my awareness of how very ancient this is, and the vastness of this web of light and wisdom that extends throughout the universe of universes. I leave this encounter and am aware of traveling at very high velocity through space. As I fly though space, stellar bodies streak by and I perceive the blackness of space and the light bodies with comet-like tails all around me. I traverse areas that are wormholes into other dimensions. These places all have different characteristics. Each recognizable, and some even familiar.

Having shed the body is such a wonderful awareness. There is no weight to lug around. I realize deeply how much energy is consumed in moving around my own small physical frame. This now shed, I am free. There are no confines. I feel in harmony. Just pure energy. There is no physical awareness. My shell lies on the woven palm mat on the floor like a log. Empty. There is no ability to move. Every reference point in my ordinary reality has dissolved.

I traverse vast distances and enter a realm that the *sabios* (the wise ones) call *el castigo*, the punishment. I am nakedly shown all the faults in my own character. Like tapping into the Akashic records, I saw specific things that I had done contrary to the Cosmic Law. The memory was burned so deep, and the feeling of remorse so great, that I cried, groaned and wailed for a very long time. It is through this experience of spiritual gnashing of teeth, the internal thrashing, that I see myself clearly. This is the purge part of purgatory. And it is the tears of heartfelt sorrow at my own actions that washes clean the spirit. Through the deep cleansing power of tears deep healing takes place.

Time has no measure, I am in the eternal, and my doors of perception know that I am dead. Like the peeling of an onion, layers of spiritual tarnish removed, and passing through this *bardo, el castigo*, emergence as if from a chrysalis happens. I am in great light, and feel merged with the sacred feminine essence, the Great Goddess, whose presence envelops me with profound love, imprinted on my essence. My deepest wish is to remain united with Her.

I am given teachings about my life, healing and Her great love for all, Her essence in all nature, the inter-connectedness of all beings, and direction on my Path. A beautiful radiant being appears and tells me that I cannot stay as it is not yet my time. I am sad at this as I do not want to return to the Earth. Accepting this command, full of love I return from the celestial dimensions, changed forever.

    My corpse like body, slowly resurrects in recognition of my holy state. All sights crystalline, and profound unspeakable love radiating from me, I return to the bare wood cabin high in the sierra, feeling blessed, healed, and joyful. The spiritual gift of the sacred mushroom medicine has been received.

CHAPTER 25 IN THE PRESENCE OF THE SACRED

Learning from the sacred mushrooms over a long time reveals many things. For the Mazatecos, and the other indigenous people that use this medicine, their experience is highly personal and not discussed openly. Only in cases of treatment of very ill people, then discussion of the medicine journey is done within the family. Otherwise the discussion is between the *sabia(o)* and the patient.

The sacred mushrooms have their own way and pace of healing a person. The *curandera(o)* is the medium of deep knowledge as to how to intuitively apply the medicine. Ignorant people think that you receive the big revelations on just one trip. In order to work with the medicine, you must obey a certain pace. This takes time. Certain diseases require a number of ceremonies.

In western society, people have been conditioned to have spirituality defined for them via an intermediary, such as a male priest. In indigenous cultures that have for millennia used entheogenic plants, there was direct contact with the divine. For organized religions, especially that of the Conquistadores that profited off the church business of intermediary between the natives and "God," it is easy to see how this could be a real threat.

When the natives not only can live in an organized society, are highly intelligent and are spiritually evolved, they were not easily convinced to change to the white man's ways. This is something that the Christian zealots can never understand. They never knew that love was the essence of the ecstasy with which these natives worshipped. When salvation is espoused based on domination and destruction, who would want it?

The sacred mushrooms are purveyors of ecstasy. It cannot be called a religion. The word religion means to regulate, to control. The sacred mushrooms are liberators. It is interesting to think about the various religious depictions so valued in western art of the saints in ecstasy. Ecstasy was that sought after. The direct contact with the divine. After all, they came over to convert the natives. And any spiritually awakened native that did not need the Catholic priests was a real threat to their power structure.

When the Spaniards did not convert through love, but rather the sword, their essential message was distrusted from the beginning. The colonizers came to pillage. They needed a large labor force to accomplish their aims in conquest. Many indigenous people were enslaved in body and mind. The destruction wrought from centuries of patriarchal colonial domination continues with the outlawing of the sacred medicines.

The sacred mushrooms through time provide us with an energetic foundation for the cornerstone of future living. They are a cosmic compass. Through their blessing, seekers are guided through the rainforest of the soul. The great spiritual laundry.

The mushroom experience is a deep womb experience for women. Not an umbilical region one, not a navel chakra one, but a womb experience. Once, on a deep journey, I felt my womb and ovaries as a generative source, better said as a power center. A major organ, a major center, pregnant with possibilities of creation.

It is a place of balance, very connected to the Earth, from which the rest of the body radiates. For a female it is like this. At times I felt that the womb energy naturally opened up my receptiveness and feelings of sexuality. It was a good feeling, a whole feeling, not a feeling driven by desire or passion. The energy running in my channels sought to connect with the same level of frequency in another.

When you are in deep ceremony, you escape from the shell of the body, and time and space are annihilated. You see with the disembodied eye the multi-colored light rays that perfume the spirit. You become aware of how heavy your body is. Senses heightened, you are a pure receptor. The visionary fields unfold, beyond thought or analysis. Your spirit is pacified by the messages contained in holy silence.

Taken to the core of your being, your entire physical, mental and spiritual self is forever rearranged. Cracking into other dimensions, regions of direct transmission, words seem so utterly useless to describe any of this. Becoming washed clean through your own tears, in an infinite ocean of love, the spirit emerges as if from a chrysalis.

We are the genetic blossoming of dreams long past. Connecting to the genetic memory of each of our spiritual legacy of the stars, encoded in the mind of nature, we are the "wild savages." The mysterious message that the star beings communicated, revealed the future of the earth and the upcoming ecological destruction, awakened a deep sense of protection for our Earth Mother.

Without any concept, the bond created through the mushroom ceremony to all elemental life was indelibly imprinted. This bond naturally formed between all those that took part in the ceremony. The element which called the most attention was water. The sweetness of water is a precious elixir. From that revelation, I have been drawn to work with water in meditation, in offerings and in healing. Attachments to material things became severed through the benefit of the view. Grasping to impermanent objects is let go. Sharing and generosity become most valuable. Beauty as supreme medicine was my prescription.

It has been shown through time that even after the greatest storm, things calm down. When you train in the medicine way life becomes close to philosophy. Searching for deeper counsel, I asked Doña Julieta about this, because she had seen so many changes in her life. She said, "*Con la vista en alto y la imaginación trabajando a todo motor,*" (Put your view high, and your imagination working at full throttle).

CHAPTER 26 THE ALLY OF TOBACCO

One spring, during some fine weather, some time after the roads were opened up, I was told that soon there was to be a big social event up at the plaza. Doña Julieta's son was the head of the youth group sponsoring the dance, much anticipated by the villagers in the region. With this honor came the obligation to feed and house the entertainment.

As I was to find out, this was no small thing. Food preparation began days in advance to make *mole negro* (black mole sauce). More than twenty ingredients had to be gathered. *Comadre* Lupe and Chavelita came daily to help, and I joined in the cooking. Many of the ingredients had to be roasted on the *comal* (clay griddle), and then hand ground on the *metate* (grinding stone).

Mole is the traditional dish made for special occasions. It is labor intensive, and really, heart feelings go into the making of it. As the week progressed, all the remaining ingredients for the dinner came together in a lovely flow.

The big day, Saturday, came. Very late in the afternoon, two pickup trucks could be heard coming up the mountain. They stopped near the house, and in came the awaited guests, the band.

Doña Julieta gave them the heroes' welcome, and the house came alive with about thirty people. As it turned out, this was not just any local group, but Reuben y Su Nuevo Sociedad, who had a claim to fame in Mexico. They had come all the way from Mexico City. Everyone in the house was excited. Darkness began to fall.

Reuben confessed that they did not think they were going to make it because the road was so bad and the village was so remote. As it was, they had to leave their large bus that they had been traveling in down by the river, because it was too big to make it up to the village.

A place to park was found, and the pickups were waiting to transport them up to the village, when they arrived. The band had already had an adventure getting there. On arrival, they were first offered the customary *trago* (drink) of *aguardiente*. This was welcomed by most of the group. The others drank some of the delicious coffee grown by Venancio.

There was enough help in the kitchen and so I was able to talk with some of the members of the band. They told me that they were very surprised to see a foreigner way up there in the mountains. They wanted to know how I had gotten there.

The food came and all of the guys became enchanted by Doña Julieta's *mole* served with turkey, rice, and hand made corn tortillas. Made with love, you could feel the afterglow of bliss waves. Everyone was content.

A few of us made it up to the walkway on the second level of the house. The night was clear and warm. In the distance the lights of Huautla shone. While talking with two of the musicians my eye was caught by something strange.

Way in the distance, a string of lights, were moving down the mountain. This seemed odd, because out there, it was wild forest. I went and asked one of the older sons about traveling lights. He said it was a cross-country race, held at night as part of the *fiesta* of the village.

I returned up to the musicians on the balcony, and watched as the lights disappeared into the blackness on the runners' uphill climb to our village. We were stargazing and enjoying the clear mountain air. The band was made up of city boys who did not make it out into distant places to play. So they were enjoying the ambiance.

Outside of the family compound, sounds of vehicles and many people chatting on foot were passing above the house going to the plaza. These kind of large dances were not often held, and so, that night was a big deal. People from the region were coming in waves.

Reuben and his boys were happy and in conversation with Doña Julieta and Venancio in the kitchen. The children were close by and listening in. It was slightly crowded, and in this charged atmosphere, everyone was feeling the elevated energy.

After a little while, the moving lights were visible in the distance heading our way. They were bobbing up and down as the runners were making their way by flaming torchlight. With the difficulty of the terrain, and at night, I mused that these runners must have cat's eyes. As they got closer to the village, people started to cheer them. The race ended up in the plaza. The crowd gave a big shout for the winner.

The band was readying for departure to set up for the event. They left some of their things behind, gathered their gear, and left the house. We could hardly catch our breath from all the action, when in came bursting through the side door a ball of energy with its own wind. This being in white was the winner of the race. And it was Doña Julieta's nephew! "*Buenas noches Tia y Tio!*" (Good Evening Auntie and Uncle).

Lithe and muscular, and drop dead gorgeous with gold teeth lighting his smile, he seemed full of energy even after this one and a half hour race. Actually the energy emanating from his body seemed to make him glow. I could not imagine how he could navigate up and down the mountain racing in the dark. His reputation had preceded him. I had heard many stories of his adventures from the family. So this is the one who is so daring, and slightly dangerous. His woven palm cowboy hat slightly cocked to one side completed the picture of this young man in his early twenties.

By winning the race, because he was a relative of the head of the sponsors for the dance, even more prestige was given to the family. Everyone was joyful at his winning and also that he came to celebrate at the house. More *mole*! The tide of the family *fiesta* was rising.

Soon thereafter, when everyone had eaten and the house and kitchen put into order in anticipation for the next round, we were told to get dressed for the dance. I got ready, and then went to Doña Julieta's room. She had put on a really beautiful dress. I saw her fiddling around stuffing something into her bra. "*Que haces Mamita?*" (What are you doing little Mother?) She looked at me with eyes of an eagle and said, "*Protección*" (protection). Protection? My mind was suspended. Protection for what???

"You need some too. Come over here!" Just then she produced a small bottle of liquid from her bosom, concealed in her dress. "We are going to a place where there are many unknown people and many eyes will be on us." She then told me to take off my top and began to rub a green liquid over my arms and belly button, while chanting.

When the liquid dried, I got dressed, and noticed that Doña Julieta had more than one bottle in her bodice. I had no idea what we were in for. All I knew is that it was the one and only time that the house was left totally alone. The entire family went to the dance.

We entered the milling crowd on the edge of the plaza that was full of people. Tables and chairs had been set out, giving a nightclub effect in front of the stage. We wound our way through the tables to the family's reserved spot. When everyone went to be seated, there was no place for me. I went to another table nearby, on the side.

I watched the scene unfold. The band began to play with people standing around, shy to dance. I felt like melting into the crowd because I was the only outsider there besides the band. When they were about to play the second song, Reuben at the mic said, "And this song is for someone special here, this is for Camila! Come on and dance!" And so, instead of melting into the crowd, there I was singled out, away from my family. And of course I had to dance. The whole family was laughing and having a good time. People got up and started to dance.

Afterwards I danced a little more, and then started to feel strange. Before, at the house when everyone was eating *mole*, I decided not to eat much because it can be heavy on the stomach. Slowly I was getting worse and worse with stomach cramps, which were intensifying. It was impossible that it was the food.

I called over Paco, and asked him if he would walk me back to the house. I was feeling pretty bad. Suspicious about what was happening, I remembered something that Doña Julieta had told me about tobacco as your ally used as a protection. I asked Paco for a cigarette. I was feeling so bad that I had to hang on Paco's arm while walking because I was bent over in pain. He lit the cigarette for me, and I puffed on it heading towards the house. I blew the smoke over myself. The pain lessened.

We got to the house and he was very concerned for me offering to stay with me instead of returning to the dance. I asked him to get me to my bed, and there I went under the covers clothed. When he closed the door to the room, I blacked out until morning.

I awoke early, and went downstairs. The band was gone. Doña Julieta said, "What happened to you?" Before I could answer, she said, "Those guys came back after playing and were up all night and then they even ate breakfast before they left!" She had not slept. I told her what had happened. She looked at me, and said, "Someone did harmful magic on you. That is why I took so much protection with me. Now you understand why I do not let you go out walking around by yourself? This place has many sorcerers! Never go out without tobacco."

CHAPTER 27   THE EMBROIDERED HUIPIL

The women of the Sierra Mazateca traditionally wear brightly colored *huipiles* (hand woven and hand embroidered "dresses"). Beneath the *huipil* a long wrap around skirt, nicely embroidered with maroon horses and designs on the hem. The simpler form of the wrap around skirt was made of blue and white horizontally striped cotton. The *huipiles* of the region are an art form using symbolic esoteric designs, many related to the sacred mushrooms.

Anyone who wears a *huipil* would certainly agree as to it being a totally comfortable piece of clothing. Made of sturdy cloth that would wear for decades, *huipiles* mostly improved with age, becoming softer and even more beautiful. There was something very special about wearing hand made cloth.

Coming from middle class USA, the clothes I had were of machine made cloth. In college, I became a life long admirer of hand woven cloth. I began to wear hand loomed skirts, and liked the quality and weight of the fabric.

Mexico has a veritable wealth of hand woven fabric of many materials. The numerous indigenous tribes each have their own regionally distinguishing *traje* (traditional clothing). Oaxaca is a special place, where a festival of folk dance of the indigenous people in magnificent colorful traditional dress is celebrated in July. Called the Guelaguetza, its pre-Columbian origin is connected to ceremonies celebrated for the corn deity and abundance from the earth.

Traveling among native people in Mexico clothed in their colorful regional dress made me realize how dull western clothing was. The further south I went the brighter the colors seemed to get. I found a simple *huipil* that I liked made in Oaxaca of hand spun white cotton thread in an unusual open weave that I call air-conditioned. Maroon designs were woven into the white, and the ample soft garment fell below my knees.

There was something about the cloth. It had a special feeling, like I was being caressed. Becoming used to this, I had an eye out for other *huipiles* to amplify my wardrobe. I began to reflect on how women in western cultures were influenced by male fashion designers to wear highly restrictive uncomfortable clothing made of non-organic materials. Native clothes were designed for function, not fashion. Clothing was modest, and this virtue among the native people was highly prized. There was none of the neurotic body consciousness with low cut and short clothes announcing " look at me."

During *fiestas*, women wore their best *huipiles*, many of them manifestations of their own fine artistry. Most of the women in the Sierra Mazateca embroidered beautifully. In procession they looked like a walking rainbow, the sun reflecting off their colorful satin ribbons.

I noticed such a big difference in worldview that these people had from the world I was raised in. My world as I was maturing was manipulated not only through clothing and style, but also right down to tight shoes, high heels, make up, and worst of all, beauty parlors. All of these factors led to a major clash for me.

The people in the village did not care about any of this stuff. It was not part of their planet. The introduction of the alien culture of the outside world came through the influence of the teachers in the school, who came from that world, sent in by the government. It was a real culture clash. They brought nail polish and make up and began to work on the young girls.

One day, one of Doña Julieta's daughters, aged eleven, came home all painted up with make up. Shocked, I said, "Who did this to you?" She said, "My teacher taught us a class in beauty." It was the teachers that started to cut the kids hair short. They had no clue as to what long beautiful hair even meant, much less what was natural beauty. These teachers from the outside had influence that affected attitudes of the population.

It was part of the indigenous culture to respect the elders. This was the social order. The elders were at the top of the hierarchy. Of course, a sign of age was the graying of hair. Because of the teachers influence, attitudes changed among the younger people who lost respect for those whose hair became gray. Because of the teachers influence, the people started to dye their graying hair black.

Doña Julieta was an adept at embroidery and sewing. She showed me a big tablecloth that she embroidered. It was for sale. So much work! I wondered how she found the time to do this. I had learned to embroider as a young woman, and greatly appreciated the handwork.

When I returned from being away for several months, one morning Doña Julieta said, "I have something for you." She produced a bag, and I opened it to see a beautiful embroidered *huipil* that she had made for me. It was such a lot of work.

She smiled mischievously and told me that I had a reminder of my initiation and work with the sacred mushrooms embroidered on the *huipil*. There were birds and flowers. It was a fantastic gift. These motifs can still be seen on the *huipiles* from the region.

I started to think about how the incursion of technology led young women away from learning any kind of handwork. There was something special about just sitting quietly with your needle, creating beauty. Working quietly embroidering or weaving, the mind goes into a natural state of peace. It is a meditative work. Quiet hands, quiet mind.

Living a simple life, time was made for doing all kinds of handwork. It took time to make your clothes. It took time to cook food. It took time to grow food. The pace was naturally slow.

When you embroider a *huipil*, it is important to have good thoughts. The thoughts go into the stitch. When you are wearing a beautiful *huipil*, you are wearing love. The embroidered *huipil* made by Doña Julieta's hands was a treasure beyond price.

CHAPTER 28   INEBRIATED WITH DEVOTION

In the morning, Doña Julieta would spend time in front of her altar praying. Usually I would stand behind her accompanying her in devotion. These moments of concentration before the images of the divine that she held dear were precious and grounding. It set the tone for the rest of the day, no matter what happened. The days usually were full with activity in the house. But there were those times, when all was quiet, and we were mostly alone, that I would ask deeper questions about the sacred mushrooms.

On one deliciously warm sunny afternoon in late spring, we sat out on the earthen patio in the cool shade. She began by saying, "The mushroom is very spiritual. When you take them, you feel in a way outside of yourself, because clearly it is medicinal. It is physical, material, and spiritual. It resolves all of the problems, such as the ones you had before. Since years before, our elders healed with this."

"There was no medicine, there was nothing. Therefore it (the sacred mushrooms) was the best medicine for everyone. For God, there is nothing occult or hidden. You have to bring out into the light what He has given you. Why? Because He makes known our soul, our spirit, our body, and for this reason you leave your body in a moment, thinking and seeing psychedelic things, in a moment!"

"As for me here in the house, which is your house, in truth you have seen that I have many patients. And these patients, well, they have become transformed within themselves. The mushrooms are really fabulous, and for me it is the great medicine of the world. Because through them we can see and take account of who we are, how we are, of what we are, and how we are made up, before God. We are shown many things about life, and the many difficulties we have to overcome. These difficulties are sufferings, sadness, sickness, among others."

"The medium of the mushrooms teach you many marvelous things. They are enlighteners because they show, they teach, the best teacher, no? The truth is it's really beautiful. Well, I like to talk with you about all this, to extend to you all of this, for us to communicate with all others that yes, we need to. The reason is because there are people that abuse Nature, that abuse us, or abuse themselves, or harm another person."

"God does not want this. What God wants is that we unite, learn the best, and take others forward. In this region the mushrooms serve us to communicate with all the living beings of astronomy, of nature, which are the mountains, lakes, clouds, and all the things that exist in life. It is a really stupendous communication, no? Because this is where you begin to be taught what is happening (in a case), because you prayed in the moment, and you communicated with all of them. So they help protect one in the moment that you need it, and also to help the other person."

I reflected on what she said, and then I asked about the essence of the sacred mushrooms and her opinion about those on the outside world who had begun to grow them from spore prints from the region. She said, "The mushrooms would not turn out the same because the earth here has a lot of power, very different than the earth in other places. This is the natural place of those mushrooms, and even though you could grow them in other places from spores, they would not be the same. Just like I have blood and someone else does also, still it's blood but we are different people. The spores would produce mushrooms, but when they produce, they would not be many like here naturally in the wild."

My question was refined further when I asked that even if the mushrooms were grown outside the region from spores collected from the region, didn't they have the same genetics and power? She responded, "Yes that is true, but if they were grown on rye or wheat, that is not the same as coming out of the earth wild from where they grow naturally. For this reason it is important not to grow the mushrooms from spores."

The growth cycle of the sacred mushrooms and the traditional ceremonies during the year were explained to me. "In the beginning of the year, which is the first of January, we celebrate. Later on the first of June, and after that the end of December. These are the dates and days most sacred to us because we invoke nature."

We propitiate nature and give thanks for what has been given to us, the bread of each day. We thank our Mother Nature in the form of the moon, because she is bringing up everything. She gives us dew, she gives us water, she gives us everything. So for me it is something great to give a flood of action of thanks. We make promises, like we light candles on the first, in the middle, and at the end of the year, so that the Light continues in the house. Because it is that Light that shows us which ever insect wishes to harm us, or whatever harm comes against us."

"I think that this is like being on good terms with the president of the republic. I want to say that one is with God and Mother Nature, no? To give an action of thanks to all the beings that surround us, no? Because they are also living beings. The mountains are living beings, although there are other phenomena, but they are living beings. The water also has its living beings. You can't bathe in the rivers in June because this is when the water has her period. All of our ancients say the same, you can't play around with water, because afterwards, an infirmity comes to you that you don't know. Then the doctor tells you that it is incurable. Why? Because it is from a phenomenon."

"Our old ones say that one crosses with nature (offends Nature), and this I have seen and cured many people from this class of infirmity. So what I think is this, look, here in the region, how good, that after so many years that you have stayed here in your humble house, with the family, so what I want is, how good, to communicate with the rest. Love one another like Christ said. For something He has us here on this Earth. We can make and destroy but later there are consequences, because it is a shame to cause harm, no? It's like, to destroy a plant, to destroy an animal, all, everything has its spirit. A little animal has its *santo* (saint). A phenomenon is also sustained by up there. Our communication with the divine is strong for this reason." Pay attention, our nature, like the rocks, the hills, this is the ribs of nature, our bones, as we say, the bones of the Mother Nature, that is giving us the bread. But we are destroying everything, yes, we are destroying everything. And like they have always said, this is going to finish.

"The world isn't going to end. What's going to end are us, yes. For God there is nothing impossible. By the medium of His marvels He has His bad things, and He does them, because it is of Him, and we are of Him, and we come from Him. It's the most indispensable thing to think about to concentrate ourselves in one moment on Him."

CHAPTER 29   THE GRINGO LEGACY

The modern story of the sacred mushrooms has to be told not as history but as herstory. We are speaking about a women's story, therefore not limited by patriarchal language, it can be said that this is herstory. It was the women that were the main players in this part of the story.

Somehow the sacred mushrooms, so well hidden, almost forgotten, touched the mind of an important, humble man, on a train going somewhere else in Mexico. Again and again I am impressed by the stories I hear. It seems like there is a subtle undercurrent of movement in consciousness, allowing the magic to spring forth.

When the original news broke to the public about the existence of the sacred mushrooms, it almost went unnoticed. Those of us who were undergrads in the seventies were enraptured by the stories of Carlos Castenada and his training with Don Juan in Mexico. Word got out about an alternate reality and those of us reading Carlitos' stories were wanting to experience it.

I had been studying with Doña Julieta in the Oaxaca *sierra* for many years. During that time, as my path had it, I was fortunate to study and practice with a great Tibetan Buddhist meditation master. My training involved the power plants and the yogas.

At one point I had heard that a great terton, a treasure revealer, from Tibet was coming to the U.S. for the first time. My teacher was sponsoring his visit. All the students were atwitter as to how their lives totally changed after meeting with him and getting his initiations. He was touring many cities giving teachings, and was nearing the end of his tour in Boston.

No matter how juicy the news was about him, the money was not there for me to travel and get his blessing personally. I was yearning to meet him, and I was thousands of miles away. So I prayed.

One day, I got a phone call out of the blue, from one of my teacher's old students. He asked me if I had seen the terton. I said that I was stuck without funds to go see him. He said, "You have to go see him. I am sending you a plane ticket."

Thunderstruck, I hung up the phone and started thinking about who I knew in Boston. I needed a place to stay. Finally it dawned on me, that some years back, while on retreat with another great Tibetan lama, I met a man from Boston. The man gave me his card, and said that if I ever came east, to please visit.

I started to look for the card, but could not find it. I checked and rechecked the book where I had put the card but nothing. Almost at the end of my patience, I started to pray, and lifted up the book turning it upside down shaking it, and the card fell out!!!

I contacted the man and arranged to stay with him and his wife. They were so interested in the story of the terton that they decided to go to the initiations with me. I went separately from them because I was going to the house where my teacher and the terton were staying, complete with entourage.

In that neck of the woods, the scene around this high lama was taken over by students of another renowned meditation master. They had taken up a way that was kind of militaristic with uniforms. When I appeared at the door of the house, arms filled with offerings, I asked to see my teacher. The guard at the door told me that I could not enter, as they were not advised anyone was coming.

I had just flown thousands of miles and gone through many hoops just to get there. I was not going to back down. Just as I was contemplating my next action, my teacher appeared from behind the guard and literally pushing him aside, opened the door and surprised to see me, so far from home, he said, "Come in!"

The arrogant guard, crestfallen, stepped aside. My teacher, a no nonsense man, told me to follow him. I was overjoyed to see my teacher. Wily and energetic as usual, he was happy I came. I told him about the plane ticket. We walked through the big old house, and he took me right into the bedroom of the terton!

There he was, a big man, with dark brown skin, and shaved head lying on the bed, smiling, receiving people. He had traveled into the western world from a wild region of far eastern Tibet and was renowned as a mahasiddha, (a miracle worker).

I was seated on the floor in front of him by my teacher. My teacher said, "Talk with him. He will appreciate a westerner who tries to speak his language." I was to be his entertainment. He looked at me, and suddenly I became mute. I could not speak at all. He laughed at me. I was glad to provide him with some humor. He then gave me his blessing.

After several days of initiations with him and hundreds of students that showed up at a large hall, this marvelous scene disappeared like a dream. I had three days left before my return, and I was asked by my hosts what I would like to do. Like a lightning bolt it hit me and I blurted out, "Harvard. Dr. Schultes. He is there. I would so like to meet him!"

My host looked at me, and said very casually, "He is a friend of mine. Would you like me to give him a call?" I was astounded. A direct connection. This was real magic. Arrangement was made for lunch the following day.

I was taken to Harvard, and really not knowing where I was on the street as we approached, I was just looking around. We walked down the street, and I was guided through a tunnel into the grounds of Harvard. It was dark like going through a birth canal. When I got through the tunnel, something overcame me, a feeling that I was in a bastion of deep knowledge. I could feel the sanctity of that knowledge. So many gifted scholars had walked in these places.

My interest was sparked as I was led through this old building, and up stairs, past a closed gate, climbing more stairs until standing in front of a closed door with a big sign pasted on it that said, "No admittance except for Dr. ......". My host knocked and then opened the door. We were expected.

Inside, behind a desk, was a tall elderly gentleman, who looked up from his many papers, over the glasses on his nose. Recognizing my host, we were cordially welcomed. I was not prepared for his most kind reception when I was introduced to him.

He was very happy that I had come, and we spoke mostly in Spanish. He decried the fact that there were not many Spanish speakers around him. Dr. Schultes was one of my all time heroes. Known as the father of ethnobotany, he was a pioneer in the study of entheogenic plants among indigenous people.

Tough as nails, he had spent a lot of time in the jungle in Columbia, collecting plants and enduring great hardship. He seemed like an ascetic. His manner was humble and endearing. Both of us shared our great love for the jungle and the many medicinal plants that grew profusely.

Our conversation took off quickly about entheogenic plants. I shared my story about my apprenticeship with Doña Julieta in the Sierra Mazateca. His eyes lit up. He seemed to be excited. He then said, "Come with me I have something to show you." Before we left his office, he gifted me one of his books on psychotropic plants. He inscribed it and I was very honored to receive it.

   I had no idea where we were going as we stepped outside of his office. Everything seemed old. The dark shelves of the filled bookcases, with only dim light filtering in, created an aura of hidden knowledge. He took me to his old classroom, which had been preserved intact like a museum exhibit. There were glass-covered cases in the room in which were many kinds of medicinal plants which he had brought back from his forays into the wild. All kinds of old indigenous objects, among which were his prized blowguns, graced the walls of the room. He pointed out some special items to me.

   Knowing that he had a kindred spirit, he then said, "Now follow me." We exited the classroom and then walked through what seemed a labyrinth to me. I was being taken into the inner sanctum of one of Harvard's true treasures. We walked and got to a locked door, which he opened with a key. Then we reached another locked door. A woman was at a desk near it. He asked her for the key, and with it we gained entrance.

   When the door opened, I stepped into the Wasson Library. The walls were covered with books on shelves. Some in boxes on the floor. On the top of the shelves were all kinds of objects from many cultures. All of the objects were sacred mushroom ceremonial objects, or depictions of the sacred mushrooms in art. There were display cases with precious rare pre-Columbian sacred mushroom artifacts.

I looked around amazed. He looked at me and smiled. I had been led into the room with the entire private collection of Gordon Wasson. Almost dumbstruck at seeing this incredible treasure, I walked around the room looking at the books and objects. Dr. Schultes looked on like a doting father.

In the glass case, one object caught my attention. It was a pre-Columbian mushroom stone. On the front a man was carved, with the mushroom behind him. I asked Dr. Schultes if I could touch it. He requested the key for the locked case from the secretary, and opened it. He smiled.

I reached into the case and took out the mushroom stone and set it down. Looking at it, I was drawn to put my hands on the cap of the mushroom. On contact, I felt a wave of an electric current pass through me. My body began to shake uncontrollably. I went into ecstasy. Waves of bliss and visions washed over me, my tears flowing.

After some time, I returned to my body and took my hands off the stone. It had felt like I had put my hands into an electric socket. I was completely disheveled. Since that time, the mushroom stones have held my interest, and I have been able to be with many of them.

Worthy of mention within that same case was a mushroom stone made of clay with a face in the stem, and another of a woman praising the mushroom before her, also made of clay. These were very unusual pieces. The mushroom stone that I touched was placed back in the case and it was locked.

Dr. Schultes invited me to lunch. We had an animated conversation. He invited me to return to have lunch again. I was delighted. In our conversation he told me about his travels with

Weston La Barre in Oklahoma, spending time with indigenous medicine men and learning about peyote in the 1930's.

The conversation was fascinating enough, but then he went on to tell me about how he found out about the sacred mushrooms of Oaxaca. He said that at the time of his doctorate he had gone to Mexico. Traveling by train between Mexico City and Oaxaca, the journey was interrupted by problems on the train tracks. The train could proceed no further. The tracks were in need of repair. And so, while stranded in a desert region, somewhere in Puebla, the passengers got off the train and waited for the repairs to be completed.

It was just this unusual occurrence which led him to one of the most important meetings of his life. On the train also was traveling another man deeply steeped in plant knowledge. Out in the desert, these two giants in ethnobotany met.

Dr. Schultes began a conversation in his poor Spanish with an elderly woman. *"Cuantos anos tiene?"* Overheard by the Mexicans, they began to laugh in an uproar. Dr. Schultes laughingly told me that his question meant to ask the woman how old she was, only as he asked it, it came out as "How many anuses do you have?" If that wasn't enough to crack everyone in earshot up, he was trumped by her answer, *"Solo uno señor"* (only one sir).

Of those who heard all this was Blas Pablo Reko, a botanist from Mexico who had studied the power plants of the indigenous people. The two men became friends and while waiting for new railroad ties to be laid down to fix the tracks, stories were exchanged about their interests. It was Blas Pablo Reko that told Dr. Schultes where the sacred mushrooms could be found. They were stranded on the tracks not far from the region of the Sierra Mazateca.

Dr. Schultes went on to describe his amazement at how the ties that were laid down to fix the tracks were made from saguaro cactus. They grew that big in the desert. The stories that Blas Pablo Reko shared enticed Dr. Schultes to soon thereafter take off on foot into the Mazateca.

In the late 1930's the only travel into the Sierra Mazateca was on a well worn path traveled for who knows how long by the local Mazatecos. Dr. Schultes gathered supplies at a town at the foot of the mountains, loaded up some pack mules and headed into the sierra. He told me it took him four days to walk to Huautla.

We parted after that great storytelling, and made an appointment to return. The next time we met, Dr. Schultes took me into the Wasson Library again. Again I wandered around soaking up the tail wind of the Wasson's many travels into the realms of the sacred mushrooms. It was Dr. Schultes' foray into Huautla and his later writing about it that got Gordon Wasson and his wife Valentina on the trail.

The impressive collection of mushroom artifacts and exquisite books was made over a period of time. And it all was because of Valentina. Gordon Wasson was a micophobe, and Valentina was a mushroom lover. She was a Russian doctor, and enjoyed mushroom hunting and lore. Valentina was who converted Gordon Wasson to the way of the sacred mushroom.

The Wassons went to Huautla, and sought out a shaman to give them a mushroom ceremony. Gordon went to the local authority to ask who might help him. The authority sent word to a humble Mazatec woman named Maria Sabina, to attend these visitors. Unknown to the Wasson's, local indigenous custom dictated that when the authorities make a request of a villager, it is considered an obligation to attend to it.

The Wassons got their ceremony, and spent a brief time in Huautla. They returned to the States and wrote an article about their experience in Life magazine in the mid-1950's. Complete with photos of Maria Sabina in ceremony, the word was let out to the world, and this opened up Pandora's Box not only for her, but for her region. It did not take too long after that article that many international seekers made the arduous journey into the Sierra Mazateca looking for Maria Sabina and a mushroom ceremony.

Her name and fame resounded within and without the republic and in short time she became very sought after. All kinds of people came looking for her, among many were hippies. By the mid-sixties, a rent in the social fabric of the traditional Mazatecos in Huautla happened with a large influx of seekers from the outside world. There was no infrastructure in the village to handle the number of people putting a strain on the authorities.

The situation reached the tipping point in 1968. Things got out of hand when freaks seen semi-naked in the streets offended the mores of the very conservative Mazatecos. And then, one day, a young man was found semi-nude and not in his right mind in the street near the market place. He had made the grand mistake of mixing LSD that he brought with him, with the sacred mushrooms.

The indigenous authorities got him. When his identity was revealed, a shock wave went through the community. He was the son of one of the most politically powerful men in Mexico. He was sent home to his parents in Mexico City.

Because of this stupidity, the entire Sierra Mazateca was sealed off by the Mexican government from 1968 to 1974 by order of President Díaz Ordaz. This caused great hardship for all of the people that lived in the *sierra*. No outsiders were allowed up into the mountains. The road was blockaded and under guard. Only locals were allowed to pass. Public transport was very limited. For years afterward, it was still hard to get into the *sierra*.

In talking story with Dr. Schultes about the region, I told him about the years of getting by the blockade traveling in the late night. Looking at the Wasson's collection, I would have loved to hear their stories. The collection was just being catalogued when we were in the library. After some time, when I was satiated, we went for lunch.

Over our last meal together, our conversation turned to the sacred plants. We were in delight. I asked him if he had ever had a mushroom ceremony. He confessed to my amazement that he had never eaten a heroic dose. He never had a direct encounter with the Great Mystery through this wondrous medicine. Our parting was affectionate.

Some years after the Wassons article in Life, Maria Sabina was interviewed by a French magazine. It was a rare interview. Of note was her final statement, after being asked her feelings about doing the ceremony for the Wassons and the resultant aftermath. "I should have said no."

CHAPTER 30 LAS CURACIONES – THE HEALINGS

Many times Doña Julieta's house was full of people. On the upper floor, a room that doubled as a storeroom, served to house patients and their families who had come from afar for treatment. Sometimes the treatments took days, and watching how and when the medicine was delivered was captivating.

So many of the treatments happened in the kitchen, that I mused that for women traditional native doctors, here was the original doctor's office. Diagnosis and treatment happened many times in the vicinity of the fire. For difficult to diagnose diseases, divination was done.

After a few years of returning to Doña Julieta's house, one spring, a mother appeared with her nine year old son who was suffering with a skin problem. It was a slightly delicate situation to examine the boy, because his problem was on his genitalia, legs and buttocks. The Mazateco are a modest people.

The child was coaxed to bare himself, and I was unprepared to see what he suffered. The poor thing had raised sores all over his noble parts, some in scabs, some open. Doña Julieta began treatment with *tepezcohuite* (a tree bark), ground up and made into a paste, then applied all over the afflicted areas. After the paste began to dry, the child seemed relieved. Later on Doña Julieta told me that there was a skin disease epidemic, something they had not seen in the region before.

I suppose it is the same for anyone starting out on the path of a healer to be a bit timid. For me there was no gentle entry. One day, people arrived from a great distance and the woman of the family was very ill. She was laid out on a *petate* in the storeroom on the bare floor up on the second story of the house. Doña Julieta was very busy that day with other people, and so, she told me to go upstairs and start treating the woman.

The room that the patient was in had faint light filtering through the open doorway. There lying before me was a small groaning woman, with her family sitting mutely near. I quietly began my work, massaging her abdomen and back. After awhile, she relaxed and stopped groaning. Then she fell into a peaceful sleep. There were no words spoken. They didn't speak Spanish anyway. She recovered after a few days, and then the family left.

I heard many stories of unusual illnesses and difficult to cure cases that Doña Julieta managed to heal. She never took credit for the healing. She would just say that it was the divine that healed. Recompense for her services many times came in the form of food, as money was always in short supply. Some patients would repay a long time later, with a chicken showing up at the house borne by a family member in thanks.

Strange illnesses manifested when people had *susto* (fright). Western allopathic medicine did not have this one on the books. It is worth mentioning however, since many people suffer from this illness. When there is a *susto*, the spirit jumps out of the body. A child was brought for healing by his mother who was beside herself with worry. Something very strange was happening to her son.

On observation, nothing seemed amiss. The mother was asked to relate the symptoms. She said that at times, grass would come out of the child's eyes. When Doña Julieta heard this, she was incredulous. The mother seeing disbelief in Doña Julieta's face then produced out of her *rebozo* a small jar filled with grass. This was proof of what came out of her son's eyes.

It was a most unusual case of *susto*. The treatments began with spiritual cleanses, then a divination, and a sacred mushroom ceremony. The child was healed.

When this story was related to me, I was astounded, and had it not come from Doña Julieta I would have said it was smoke. She showed me the jar of grass as proof. What was mind-bending were the types of symptoms that *susto* caused. If that case was not surprising enough, Doña Julieta told me another story.

Once a mother appeared overwrought about her son. He was really sick and she had not been able to get him healed. It was during the cold time of the year. Doña Julieta asked the mother about her son's symptoms.

The woman began to relate that one day she noticed something had happened to her son and he did not seem to be very present mentally. She then related that afterwards, he had started to eat blankets (these were hand woven wool blankets). He unraveled the threads and consumed a blanket.

"He ate a blanket?" said Doña Julieta. The mother, who had been concentrating on the interview, looked over at her son, and said, "Just like he is doing now!" And there he was sitting and eating his blanket number two.

What could have caused this? A divination was done, and treatment begun. This was a difficult to cure case. However, with a sacred mushroom ceremony that was done, he became well again.

These stories were so astounding that I began to ask more detail of how to handle these kinds of cases. Doña Julieta told me that there are many strange things in nature. Anomalies. These kinds of cases are medical anomalies. She also went on in detail of what causes *susto*.

Of most interest was what she related about offending the spirits, and the elements. Clumsy thick-brained humans hardly acknowledge that these beings exist. However, in truth you can get really sick if you cross these beings.

And so she told me to walk very carefully on the Earth, observing everything. You have to honor the elements, and Mother Earth. Never pee in a river, ocean, lake, on a tree, or on a rock, especially the big ones. More than one indigenous system of traditional medicine speaks of this. It is called crossing the Mother Earth.

There were so many kinds of healings that took place at the house. Among those which were really quite astonishing to witness were the extractions. Of the great gifts that Doña Julieta possessed was that she was a "sucking doctor." This kind of treatment was very difficult to master. One had to have great breath control and concentration.

What was out of the ordinary for me was daily occurrence there. Being in that house was stepping through an invisible portal into the great Other. I was privileged to be a witness to something that was disappearing.

CHAPTER 31 RECONNECTING WITH THE ANCESTORS

Harvest time is a beautiful time in Oaxaca. The weather is excellent, with warm sunny days. It is a time of the biggest *fiesta* of the year, *El Día de los Muertos* (The Day of the Dead). It is celebrated in two days of remembrance on the first and second of November. The origin lies in ancient native roots and is part of the cycle of corn. At this time of the year, the veil between worlds is very thin. It could be said that in these regions where custom is strong, you can feel it.

Corn is planted in order to have a harvest to feed the dead. It is a joyful celebration, an annual remembrance and veneration of the ancestors. To the western educated mind, this seems strange if not crazy. Especially when you witness the amount of sacrifice, saving, and labor that goes into making offerings for the ancestors.

However, what is really strange is how western culture has lost this important and essential thread of remembrance. A total disconnect. I received loving guidance from my Tía (auntie) in the mountains over a number of years, which opened the door to the celebration of the Day of the Dead.

She took me under her wing, and instructed me in the making of *mole negro* (black mole sauce), and *tamales* both sweet, with meat, and herbs. This was all time consuming work with everything ground by hand, and prepared over the fire. It took days. This had to be the real origin of slow food.

These preparations were begun months before, with raising the turkey that would be sacrificed for the celebratory meal. Turkeys were considered sacred animals. People would save for the whole year to buy the necessary offerings for the dead. Everyone who lived in the countryside maintained this tradition.

Starting with the cooking, it was a real process. First the wood had to be cut in the forest, hauled by burro or horse, or on a man's back, then split, ending up in the kitchen. Both men and women were good with the axe and machete.

A trip to the market, held once a week, was needed to buy the ingredients: dried chilies, chocolate, seeds, sugar, herbs and fruit. We traveled by pickup over bumpy dusty roads leaving early in the morning to get the best of the great variety available. It was a high time in the market. All the merchants, mostly colorfully dressed women, had their goods spread out on tarps on the ground. The men were the merchants in the dry goods store. People were bustling around bargaining.

I would follow behind Tia in the market, squeezing through the press of people there doing the same thing we were. Many villagers came in from distant places on foot to this market. It was a fun and festive atmosphere. I got to carry the bags containing the selected ingredients.

Besides the makings for the *mole*, what was considered very special was the bread of the dead. These were round breads made with the form of a face in it, or sometimes made into the form of a person. The bread was made with eggs, and it was delicious and sweet. The bread was placed as an offering on the altar.

Two days before the celebration, the *mole* started to be prepared. There were so many ingredients, many toasted over the fire on a *comal*. Making *mole* is the true meaning of slow food. Grinding in the same way that the natives did in pre-Columbian times on the *metate* (grinding stone) took a lot of time. When you witnessed how much energy and time it took to make the exquisite dish, you learned to appreciate food.

You have to have good thoughts as you make the *mole*. Your heart has to be happy and pure to make this offering for the ancestors. In addition to making the *mole*, corn was cooked and ground to make tortillas and *tamales*. Beautiful white corn that my Tio (uncle) grew was an essential part of these offerings.

The *milpa* (cornfield) was located forty-five minutes walking down the mountain. The beautiful corncobs in quantity, hauled in strong expandable hand twined string bags made of *maguey* fiber, were brought up by burro. Everyone was happy seeing the burro arrive with the harvest. What a good feeling!

The large brown clay *ollas* (pots), wide and deep, sat on top of the wood fire. Within, when the *olla* was hot enough, the ingredients of the *mole* were put in. Little by little, elegantly stirred with hand made wooden spoons, until a rich dark brown, almost black, medium thick sauce was rendered.

On October 31, the whole family gathered to participate in making the altar for the ancestors. The women all were artists, and so, some of the adornments were very clever, such as garlands of peanuts in the shell, tied with hard candies. These hung from the rafters of the room in front of the altar. The men made an arch out of *carrizo* (a type of cane). This then was tied to the altar, and then the women worked together to tie flowers and fruit to the arch.

The flowers were orange marigolds, the flowers of the dead. Other wildflowers were used such as *pericon* (tagetes lucida), a lovely orange yellow that abounds in the mountains. Many kinds of fruits were integrated into the flower design on the arch. Bananas, apples, lime, loquats, and in some areas *jicamas*, were hung from the arch.

When this act of creative inspiration was complete, the rest of the altar was made. These altars were made in tiers, and so it had a stair step look. Sometime there were two levels and sometimes three. All were covered by a tablecloth, and then the multitude of offerings was artistically placed. Of importance was a plate of turkey with *mole, tamales, mezcal,* and tobacco. The final result was that everyone was content with their co-creative effort which took many hours. Thus, the single components were magically blended to create the transformation of the finished product of an altar into a portal for the ancestor spirits.

The nights are clear at this time of the year with magnificent stars. Once I arose early before dawn, and came down to the altar to meditate. A friend, Renie, accompanied me. I lit the candles, and we sat on the floor before the altar to meditate. Above the altar, some small breads in the form of people were hanging among the other adornments.

We made prayers for the ancestors and burned *copal* as the light changed in the sky. Then we sat in meditation for awhile. There was no sound. Everything was still. Just as we were coming out of meditation, one of the little people breads fell down right in front of me. We turned to look at each other, and smiled. There was no way that the bread could have come loose. It was tied up there. Tia always told me that the ancestors left signs on or around the altar. I have seen many times when some of the offerings were visibly partially consumed.

The next day, we arose at the same hour to once again meditate in front of the altar. Seated in the darkness, with dim candlelight, we meditated until past dawn. Everything was silent. We felt such a calm and warm presence. Then one of the breads fell right in front of Renie. Again we looked at each other in disbelief, and then started laughing.

When the family started to arrive, we told Tia what happened. She smiled knowingly. Then the day started in her own special way, offering us sweet tamales made by her loving hands, and hot chocolate.

Customs vary in the villages, but in general, November 1 and 2 are days of deep remembrance. This includes visiting the graves of the ancestors in the local graveyard, and cleaning the graves. This activity is always poignant, as it connects you with the person in the grave. It allows you to know that you too will die, and it could be soon.

Being physically present in the graveyard, in the company of family members and other villagers who are engaged in the same activity is a deeply bonding experience. We walked in single file procession, some family members carrying brooms and buckets of water, some carrying armfuls of flowers, and candles. Everyone was cleaning the tombs and sometimes weeping, greeting other villagers who they haven't seen in awhile, some returning from working in distant lands. All hearts and minds focusing on the departed, and honoring them.

Customarily in the village, the spirits are called in at mid-day on November 1 with fireworks. Then the family gathered at the altar, and lit bees wax candles and *copal*. As the delicious smell of this ancient resin filled the room enticing the spirits to come, prayers were made for the ancestors. When the long prayers were finished, family and friends hugged, special homage being paid to the living elders, and the *fiesta* started with a ceremonial toast of *mezcal* and followed by feasting on *mole*.

These two days were generally spent visiting and feasting. No work is done. A celebration is held in the cemetery on Nov. 2. People come out dressed in their best. On November 2 after mid-day, offerings from the altar were given away to the visitors. This food exchange was a binding factor in the community. Food was exchanged between the living and food was exchanged between the living and the dead. The spirits were sent away with another volley of fireworks again at mid-day. On the night of the 2nd there was a dance in the village.

The beauty created for the ancestors caused a rebirth in me. Something that had been almost forgotten somehow got reignited. This was Tia's gift to me. Through the remembrance of this practice, not only in mind but in action, it has brought great peace, joy, richness, wonder, and contentment to me and all those who this touches. Many times Doña Julieta would tell me, "We are only a few ounces of dust and ash."

CHAPTER 32   THE JOURNEY NORTH

During my years of apprenticeship with Doña Julieta, I had the wish that she could come to the U.S. to teach about the sacred mushrooms. I made many requests to her, telling her about how many people had interest in the medicine. Each time I asked her about traveling, she only smiled.

Seeing the amount of daily work on her shoulders, it was difficult for her to get away. I discussed bringing her north with her husband. He asked me why I wanted her to come. I said so she could teach. "She doesn't have anything to teach. Besides there is nothing up north only pure desert."

I looked at him incredulously. His opinion about what existed in the north was based on a journey he once took to the north of Mexico, where true, there is a lot of desert. As far as what Doña Julieta had to teach, he had not much value for her knowledge.

Because of his attitude, I doubled my effort to get her out of the village. This took collaboration, and I enlisted my brother Jimmy for help. He was very kind acting as intermediary when I needed backup dealing with her husband. Besides getting permission from her husband to leave, there was the giant issue of getting a passport and a visa.

I was on hold for this for many years. And then one day Doña Julieta announced that she had a vision and was instructed to journey north with me. One cannot conceive of how much red tape and difficulty, including a lot of money, it was to get Doña Julieta her passport and visa. It meant several journeys to the far distant capital to government offices. This took a lot of time and big effort.

Finally when the papers came through, quite miraculously, she got a ten year visa. I was elated. I began the movement to bring her into the United States. This took much planning and contacts. We decided that the best time of the year to come would be wintertime, because her duties in the house were lighter. Coffee harvest wasn't until early spring, so there was a window of time open for her to travel.

Our journey began on the feast of the Three Wise Men, January 6th. We decided that it would be an auspicious day to enter the USA. Our plane left Mexico City at night. We walked through the airport, and noticed a statue of Xochipilli, the deity connected with psychotropic plants on exhibition.

Finally we boarded the plane and I made sure that she got the window seat. She was apprehensive but adventurous as we took off. We got to altitude and she looked out at the inky blackness of the night and the many stars. Her face was radiant and she turned to me and smiled and said, "Can we open the window?"

We flew for hours and this whole experience was one of discovery of new things in the outside world for Doña Julieta. Landing in Arizona, we waited in line for Customs. She was very happy and spoke with the people in line near us. "This is my first time in America!" she said happily. A female Immigration officer came by us in the line and stopped near us. "This is my first time in America!" she said again to the officer.

In the moment I did not know how to react, so I just kept quiet and watched. Fortunately the officer was a bit bemused by her words. She smiled. We got up to the front of the line and Doña Julieta went through first. I made prayers that all would go smoothly. She passed through easily.

My turn came and as I moved forward to the officer, Doña Julieta waited just beyond at a relatively close distance. The officer looked me over and entered my info in the database. Then instead of being allowed through, the officer had me wait there. He called his superior.

I was wondering what was going on, as my papers were in order. They started to question me. Remaining calm, I answered, and then looking at Doña Julieta, I gave her a sign that there was a problem. Weighing the moment, I decided to speak up. "What seems to be the problem, officer?" "Have you crossed the border here in the past few months?" "No sir." They looked at me. Just then out of the corner of my eye I saw Doña Julieta blow on them from behind.

"Surely there are not two people with the same name and the same passport number…" I said. Just then they handed me my passport and let me through. I was the last one of the passengers from that flight to make it out. Doña Julieta smiled at me and asked what happened. That was our entrance into the USA.

On this journey there were many firsts for Doña Julieta. Like learning to navigate sliding doors and escalators. The journey took a lot of coordination and collaboration from many people. We began in Arizona, traveled to California, New Mexico and finished in Texas.

During six weeks of intensive travel, there were many medicine ceremonies, talks and healings done. Special ceremonies for the Mother Earth happened in Esalen and in New Mexico. Everyone benefited from her presence.

In northern California, we did a few ceremonies. As the magic flowed, connections were made and to our delight we met Dr. Tom Pinkson and the Wakan community. We spent some excellent time in teaching in the open air at Slide Ranch on the grassy cliff edge above the blue Pacific. Sue who lived there went into false labor and Doña Julieta knew just what herbs to pick for a tea to calm her and keep the baby in.

A small group of people gathered one very stormy night in the San Geronimo Valley for a *velada*, an all night ceremony. It was the first time that this sacred ceremony was given in California. It was beautiful and very intense at times, with some big healing coming from it. This event was commemorated by Tomás Pinkson in his Gifts From the Brown Madonna, Stories from Grandfather Fire. The beauty way of friendship and support from Tomás and the Wakanistas continues until the present.

The journey was not easy. During a ceremony, there was a hair-raising encounter with a powerful spirit that took possession of Doña Julieta. A battle ensued with the spirit to rid it from her. Fortunately we were accompanied by a wise male companion who was also a healer. He helped me in the intensity, and assisted us to flee that place. Driving down the mountain, a bobcat came in front of us, and then bounded into the brush.

I called a friend who lived nearby and requested sanctuary, telling her what happened. We holed up in Palo Alto for awhile. I called my *hermano mara'akame* Tomás Pinkson who had helped us in our Marin activities to come do some healing on her. The spirit had displayed strange behavior in her and she was energetically very vulnerable.

After a few days of total rest, she recovered. We traveled south down the beautiful California coast, towards our next encounter at Esalen. Taking our time traveling, nearing sunset found us on the coast near Big Sur. We stopped on the side of Pacific Coast Highway and got out of the car to see the sun go down. There was no wind and it was perfect temperature. The sky got red as the sun started to touch the horizon.

Then, as if by magic, the sun took the form of a big mushroom as it went down. Our protector, C. Jay, looked at me with an open mouth. My mouth was open too. Unbelievable! Doña Julieta just laughed at us with a twinkle in her eye.

We spent several glorious days at Esalen, healing in the exquisite thermal spring waters there. Many years before I had the intuition that I had to bring her to that place. Then, when we did our first teaching in Arizona, we met C. Jay, who later turned out to be our protector, and was a most excellent healer at Esalen. I explained my vision of her being at Esalen. He made all the arrangements.

Through Doña Julieta's vision, she said that a ceremony needed to be done there. And so, several people came to help gather the necessary offerings. Early one morning, we did the ceremony of paying the Earth. It was the first time that this ceremony had been done in the United States. We all were very moved. It was very special making that magical connection with C. Jay and we were so happy and delighted to have him near.

We had been on the road for several weeks and Doña Julieta was starting to get home sick. There were several weeks of activities still to come. So far we had been favored by a mild climate, but that was soon to change.

CHAPTER 33   INCIDENT AT CHIMAYO

The next to the last stop of the journey after many trials and tribulations was in Santa Fe, New Mexico. We arrived in very cold weather. As we were being taken from the airport in Albuquerque up to Santa Fe, snow began to fall. This is the first time Doña Julieta had ever seen snow, so it was really a wondrous thing to her.

The trip was pretty tiring and we napped along the way. As we were being driven, stories were told to us about how, at that time, the last hearings in the court in New Mexico were about to begin regarding the legality of the use of peyote, especially for the Native American Church. We also heard that Doña Guadalupe, Huichol elder, and a shamaness from Mexico, was in Santa Fe to support the medicine, so that the law would be in favor of all those that wish to participate in the sacred sacraments.

I was very joyful to hear about this and knew of the importance of Doña Guadalupe being there. This elderly grandmother was one of the few shamaness lineage holders of the sacred medicines in Mexico. It had been explained to us that there would be a welcoming celebration for Doña Julieta that evening and we were also told that Doña Guadalupe would be there. Doña Julieta was happily looking forward to meeting Doña Guadalupe. After a brief rest in Santa Fe, we got ready for the evening. Dressed in our ceremonial *huipils*, we were taken by car out to a place where the reception was being held.

The snow had continued to fall and by the time we had arrived at the house, there was about four to five inches of snow on the ground before dusk and so it was quite wondrous for us to see. We went inside and were received by the people and slowly, slowly other Native people arrived and a few other people from the community.

A little before the welcoming ceremony began, Doña Guadalupe and Doña Julieta met. In that instant when they greeted one another, I was aware that I was witnessing a unique moment in time. Everything seemed suspended, a time warp. Two of the great shamanesses of Mexico, lineage holders of the two great medicine ways, the peyote medicine and the sacred mushrooms were exchanging *kupuri* (Huichol for life force – energy). That they were meeting under these circumstances, what great fortune! In that moment of recognition in their eyes, the divine radiance of their smiles said it all. I was amazed at this opportunity that I was being afforded to be in the same room with the both of them. Everyone was touched. It was a herstoric moment.

As the evening continued, I introduced myself to Doña Guadalupe and translated for both of them for a good part of the evening. The lengthy ceremony was done by a native man who spoke in English. That evening was spent in good company with a lot of very soulful people who were there to not only welcome Doña Julieta, but also to bask in the incredible light of both of these exceptional women.

The snow continued to fall outside and we decided to leave early because of the condition of the roads. When we came outside the snow had gotten much deeper and we were in a winter wonderland. Returning by car to our place for the night was a slippery ride. The roads were deep in snow and I was worried that we would get there safely. When we arrived and stepped out of the car, Doña Julieta's eyes got really big because she had never seen this much snow.

I took her in the house and told her that we needed to go outside. We went into the bedroom and changed into outdoor clothes. I bundled her up in my jacket, pants, and boots and went out into the falling, silent, snow, all alone. I got her onto a country road where the houses were not too close together. We walked silently, dimly illuminated by streetlights as the snow fell softly.

Enticed by the magic of the scenery, as if a wand had been waved, we broke out in laughter and played. I showed her how to run and catch snowflakes on her tongue. We both had a marvelous time, running around in the night, doing this in the deliciousness of the down falling snow.

She had never worn boots or gloves or hats like this, or big down jackets so that she wouldn't be cold, so it was quite a sight to see her dressed like this and running around catching snowflakes on her tongue. We continued to play down the street in the snow and made snowballs. We had a mini snowball battle out in the dark, really going for it, releasing some travel tension. It was good! And it was fun.

We came upon beautiful pine trees whose branches had inches of snow piled up and we ate snow off of the branches. She stuck her face into the snow and licked the branches. Finally, because of the cold, we walked through the snowstorm and went back to the house as the snow continued to blanket everything.

In the morning when we awoke, the sun had already done its work melting the snow of the night before. Many icicles had formed off the roof of the house and on many of the plants surrounding the house. We went outside and marveled at the icicles. She had never seen ice like that before and so we took turns sucking on icicles. Everything seemed new, a new climatic experience.

That day we were taken to some native ceremonial lands in the Santa Fe area and drove through small pueblos heading out to an ancient site. We stopped along the road spontaneously. The sky was gray and looked heavy like it was going to snow again. We decided to play in the snow for a while and again had a wondrous snowball battle.

After driving for some time, we finally arrived at some ancient cliff dwellings where we marveled at the size and scope of what the ancients had done. We were impressed by what a beautiful way they had lived even in that very cold climate. We walked around and saw the ladders made out of huge logs that extended well over twenty feet up, for the inhabitants of those cliff dwellings to go from one level to another. It was quite beautiful and spectacular.

The following morning we got up before dawn and took off in the dark to go to the early morning Mass at Chimayo. The road was very lonely going out there. We were the only car traveling at that hour. By the time we arrived in front of the *Santuario*, light had started to dawn. We entered through the outer door into the foyer and early morning Mass had already begun.

As we entered, there were very few people, a handful, perhaps four, not including the priest. The interior of the place with its very unusual paintings was illuminated by disturbing bright lights. We sat to the rear, and as the proceedings went on, Doña Julieta began to do an act of penance within the Church. During the majority of the Mass, she stayed on her knees on the rock floor and rocked forward on her knees, praying. The floor was very cold and very hard and she continued like this for a very long time.

Finally when the mass was over and the people began to file out, I asked the priest if it would be possible for us to stay, the three of us, our driver, Doña Julieta and I, to meditate for a while in the church and to go into the *Santuario*. He agreed, and told us to turn off the lights as we left. When all people had departed and the church was still, we sat in front of the altar in the first pew and made prayers. There were two altars, a lower and an upper, each adorned with candles and a few trappings.

When our prayers were finished I motioned for Doña Julieta to come into the actual *Santuario* on the side of the altars. There at the back was a small room with a hole dug in the earthen floor, in which was a small mound of loose earth. The earth here was said to have healing powers. Inside of that room were all kinds of holy pictures on the walls. This place was a very, very old place where a lot of miraculous things had occurred, especially healings due to the earth in that spot.

There was an anteroom in front of the actual *Santuario* where there were many objects that healed people had left there in honor of that place. Among them were crutches, canes, and many *retablos*, small paintings that were made of cases that had been cured through the intercession of prayers being made in that place or from the ingestion of the earth in that place.

The anteroom, dimly lit, was a long room that on both sides had pictures of many different saints, as well as photos of many people who had been healed with prayers of thanksgiving underneath them. Doña Julieta motioned for me to come out into the main chapel and I went out following her and she looked at me. She had gone over to make some prayers and put in some money, I noticed, into the donation box beneath one of the places that had candles lit, a place for petitions. Then she came over to me kind of hurriedly and said "The candles, the candles, grab the candles off of the altar. I need them."

I knew our driver who was watching from the sidelines became mentally shocked when she asked me to take the candles off the altar, him being an ex-Catholic, still with those Catholic imprints on his mind. In that moment I was thrown into a quandary because here we were in a Catholic church, and I was being asked to take the candles off the altar. I confronted the question within myself "Was this an act of theft or stealing in relationship to some other shamanic work that was to be done?"

In that instant for me it was a test of sink or swim, and so, going against what was in my gut of not touching anything that was on that altar, I took both of those candles and proceeded after her quickly into the anteroom of the *Santuario* where all of the crutches and canes were hung. I looked at her and I said "But Mamá, I don't think it's such a good idea to use these candles off of the altar" and she said, "Look, I put enough money in that donation box to pay for lots of candles, I need those candles right now." And so, I acquiesced and handed them over.

She took them out of my hands and very quickly, began to work furiously, rubbing the candles on all of the holy pictures, wiping them down as it were. She was reciting many prayers and being very one pointed in her concentration of gathering energy off of the holy pictures and into the candles. I watched her and followed her around with intent. She gave me two candles and instructed me to do the same thing. And so, after the whole room was complete, not one picture either in the *Santuario* or in the anteroom, left undone, we came away with our charged candles.

I looked around for our driver and he was nowhere to be found. I realized he had left the church freaked out because of what he had witnessed. And so, we went to the car and found him in the parking lot outside. I thought that since this fellow had been so interested in shamanism, in this moment he didn't have his wits about him to stick around when the real action was happening. I felt sorry for him that he had missed an interesting opportunity. We got into the car and nary a word was said as we drove off into the early morning, down the winding country roads from Chimayo to Santa Fe.

It was a day to be remembered. All of this had caused me to deeply reflect in my mind about the ways of working, the ways of power and energy in relationship to certain spaces. Doña Julieta had asked me to cross over a line that was not very clear in my mind, and only in crossing it did I get onto the other side of my own concepts.

There was a concept of taking something, at first, from a place that was considered to be a special or sacred place. However, being open and realizing that actually this particular way of knowing, of being able to charge candles in these kinds of specific places where a lot of healing is done, is a very shamanic thing, and it's also a very spiritual thing.

What Doña Julieta in essence did, was to take hold of the energetic resources that were available as they appeared, and use them in a very quick way to gather excess energy for storage to use in future healings. Knowing that this was actually the case was what allowed me to move forward without any further hesitation to assist her. Knowing that she full well knew what she was doing. And I, as her student, had to let go of all of my concepts, had to move forward, trusting that she was guiding me in a good way. I recognized this under further scrutiny of the entire situation, of how we must take a close look at relative and ultimate truth.

Our driver, I realized on the other hand was completely caught up in all his concepts, unable to see how this kind of activity, the taking of the candles from an altar was actually used for the positive. I realized that these are the kinds of spontaneous skillful means that one gets a chance to witness on rare occasion. I was impressed by her impeccability in getting exactly what she wanted and being able to recognize that all of the elements were there and ready for her for what her necessities were in her healing work.

I realized that I had to cut through all judgment in that moment in order to come to further understanding as to what the true reality was. I was having to cut through all my pre-conditioned concepts. I wondered if the driver ever cut through his, seeing that he was interested in these same paths of power.

Through the cold of winter, the magic in one of the corners of New Mexico was harnessed, and transported to the Sierra Mazateca. In this way, the ancient tradition of shamans that traveled, that which brought energetic elements from afar to their people, was continued. The web of energy between north and south was strengthened.

CHAPTER 34   ENDURANCE COUNTS

Our journey north had been eventful. We met hundreds of people and did many healings and ceremonies. It was good.

The last place we visited was Austin, Texas, where there was a fine gathering of people. We were close to the border of Mexico and Doña Julieta had a number of local people who spoke Spanish come to meet her.

Texas is a wonderful place, and its' old Mexican population had an inherent respect for a *curandera*. Many people came for healings and we got to rest a little. It was nearing the end of the journey, which by this time had grown very long.

She was counting the days to departure, when an unusual case occurred. A gifted artist who suffered from epilepsy asked for a healing. And so, we did a *velada* for him.

As we began the ceremony in the evening, Doña Julieta gathered the ceremonial elements, among which I noted was a bottle of tequila. Besides our *copal* and tobacco, she had requested one of my red macaw feathers. This was unusual.

I was in for a big learning experience. Since we were at the end of a long and sometimes arduous journey, we were tired. But as things work, usually these are times when you get tested and called on energetically to go the extra mile.

And so it was. The ceremony went well enough for a while, and then turned highly dramatic, with the man going into full grand mal seizure. Writhing on the floor and foaming at the mouth, he looked so pitiful. We worked on him intensively for a long time until his seizure passed.

When his body was calm, Doña Julieta handed me the bottle of tequila and said, "Take a good drink of this!" I did and she soon followed me. The tequila was our medicine to calm the internal energetic.

We sat by candlelight, as the time flowed on, with only the sounds of the night creatures in the forest below. Our hearts turned to prayer for our brother and after awhile he started to come around. Soon he was sitting up and looking energized.

He became fascinated with the candle, and Doña Julieta put it before him and gave him some healing words. Then she took the red macaw feather and handed it to him. When he touched it, something happened to him. Something deep got released. He became blissful, staring into the candle, seeing what we could not.

We continued to pray, witnessing the healing. He soon relaxed and laid down to sleep. We said prayers of thanksgiving for the ability to serve in ceremony and for the healing. Almost energetically spent, we lay down, all sleeping together on the floor. Dawn came, and we slept through.

Early morning found us in peaceful repose, waking gently together. I sat up and looked at the room. It looked like a big fight had taken place, with things strewn everywhere. We had fought for his spirit. He kept his red macaw feather that was mangled from his handling.

The day of departure had arrived and we said goodbye to our Austin posse. Doña Julieta wanted to visit her son who was living in Monterey, northern Mexico, and so we flew there. On arrival, she was very excited to be back in Mexico. Homesickness had gotten the best of her. She had never been away from home for so long.

Her husband had left the Sierra Mazateca and came by bus to Monterey to meet her. There was a big reunion and celebration with her son and extended family. We stayed a few days, and I was getting increasingly uncomfortable being around too many people in close quarters and a big family scene. I couldn't get out of there fast enough.

We flew to Mexico City, and it was Venancio's first time on a plane. I had to explain things to him about flying, and the toilet. He was mystified. He did okay flying and it was not too long of a flight. Once in Mexico City, we made it to stay at one of the extended family member's house.

Doña Julieta promptly got absorbed into family politics. I was almost not in my body. Too many people tipped my inner scale, and I escaped the house and went to a museum. Drinking in the medicine of art, I decided to leave the city at once and seek refuge with friends on the coast of Oaxaca.

I went out and bought a plane ticket for the next morning. Returning to the house at night, Doña Julieta was surrounded by family members and so when there was a moment, I announced that I was leaving the next morning. She did not want me to leave and wanted me to come back to her village with her.

I told her I was leaving and that she had her husband to accompany her. She was not pleased. I was not sure what she had up her sleeve. Before I left the house that day, I caught wind that there was something going on at the family house up in the *sierra*. There was a phone call with some news earlier. Doña Julieta was disturbed.

I knew that there were family politics involved and that I was not going to have any part of it. I had to take care of myself. That night, I had a strange dream, a lucid dream that someone was sent to keep me from leaving.

In the morning, I decided to leave very early. I made my farewells, leaving Doña Julieta in the hands of her family. Out on the street, I caught a cab and made it to the airport. When I sat in my seat on the plane, I felt free. It had been a big responsibility.

Reaching Puerto Escondido, I got a hotel, and completely exhausted, began some serious healing work on myself. My body was so tired. I called on my friends Pati and Alejandro at their beautiful hand built healing place, Temazcalli. These wonderful healers completely took care of me, reviving me with massage, *temazcals* and good food.

Their kind and loving presence has been wonderful over a friendship of many years. We meditated and danced together. On Sundays we would go on day trips to distant beaches, where once they gave me a most altering *watsu* experience in an estuary by the mouth of the ocean.

I spent some weeks reviving my energy with my friends by the Pacific. Evening sunsets on the beach, long walks, meditation, and retreat. After a long journey, I was blessed with spring renewal.

CHAPTER 35 RETURNING TO THE SIERRA

The journey north with Doña Julieta completely altered my living situation. Returning to the States, I packed up my things and moved back to California. En route, I went on driveabout through the Southwest, just following my own nose and the energetic. It was most excellent affording me to see one of the natural wonders of the world, Carlsbad Caverns in New Mexico. Off season, I wandered leisurely through the depths of our Earth Mother in awe of her creations below ground.

It was late in the day, nearing closing time, and the ranger told me to sit outside the mouth of the cave to see a wonder. There were about twenty of us that sat and waited as the light started to change. The hue of the sky progressed to blue purple. Slowly, here and there came out fast flying black objects. It was hard to distinguish what they were at first because they flew so fast. And then, like a faucet being turned on to a fast flow of water, out came in swirling clouds thousands, tens of thousands, who knows what uncountable number of bats, flying up and up turning and turning.

Looking like great funnels of moving black mass, large numbers of them flew off in one direction, and then the next large emergent swirl would take off in another direction. I could feel the wind from their wings. And so it was watching these massive swirling clouds of bats as the sky changed from dusk to starlight. The bats continued to come out, almost indistinguishable from the night sky.

This led me to a bat meditation, on how these amazing creatures that few people consider, perform an astounding feat in nature of eating masses of insects and pollinating many plants. Each bat clan within the caves had their specific direction to fly into for the night harvest. Witnessing this, made me think of being taken to something special and unforeseen on my journey. This is what I call the magic of the road.

Like a doctor taking a pulse, I traveled into northern California, feeling out a new place to settle. I landed with friends in the Bay area. After a number of months the opportunity arose to return to Mexico. I jumped at the chance. I had been staying in a relatively densely populated area and was yearning for the wilds.

I was met at the airport by my *hermano* Jimmy and warmly welcomed back to Mexico City. We left the next evening and drove to the *sierra*. Our conversation on the road was long, with a recap of the journey north with Doña Julieta. The country roads were empty.

Talk turned to our travels. The sinuous dirt road into the *sierra* had been under construction for over ten years. As usual on those roads one had to expect the unexpected.

Much to our delight, our journey proceeded unimpeded, and by the time we reached the Plan de Guadalupe, daylight had broken. As we passed through the apparently deserted streets, slowly we saw signs of people beginning their day. It was a beautiful dawn, calm and clear. A chill was still in the air.

We began our descent through many curves on the road and finally came to the river. That river was like a threshold into an inner world. It was an artery of life. A liquid flowing welcome into this magic land.

We followed the river and then began to climb up to the village.

From the river's edge, I looked up the mountain at the road, and my mouth fell open. There coming down was a microbus, and the road was paved.

"A microbus!" I shouted to Jimmy. "The road is paved!!!!!" I shouted again. My eyes were wide with disbelief. I was in shock. He looked at me with compassion.

We looked at the microbus negotiating a notorious curve in the road, where a spring, emerging from the steep side of the mountain, constantly caused landslides since long time before, preventing crossing especially in the rainy season. For years, I had traversed that curve, sometimes on foot across that dangerous landslide in the mud. The villagers had been living with that landslide as part of the nature of the mountain.

I was witnessing what some people might call progress. For me the great shock was that the road up to the village had been paved. That road, unforgettable as the last steep obstacle after an arduous journey, was reason to feel the great inner hallelujah arriving and walking through the gate of Doña Julieta's house.

More than once, visitors were turned back by that curve. And now, I was witnessing public transportation coming down the mountain. Unbelievable. Something had radically changed.

When we walked through the door, we were warmly received. There was much to talk about. More big news for the village was that a telephone had been put in. Now with a new road and communication, village life was permanently altered from its original pace.

Our journey north had opened up a new world for Doña Julieta. From our hard work, enough money had been saved to realize a long time dream of hers. She took me upstairs to show me her new pharmacy that she had put in. Glowing with accomplishment, she had realized building from scratch a room that contained medicines for the village where before there was nothing.

I understood the importance of this time and so called all her daughters and granddaughter to come for a photo of that herstoric moment. Posed behind a glass case, they looked content. The fruit of much labor was so sweet.

Jimmy and I basked in the glow of this great accomplishment. Doña Julieta and her family were happy. We stayed for several days and continued to perceive the changes that had come about.

Firewood had been difficult to get. Farmers were leaving their land. Some had stopped planting all together, or were limiting their planting. Coffee prices had dropped radically and many farmers were affected. Farmers were seeing the effects of pesticide use on the environment.

When farmers stopped planting, this changed the economy and forced the local indigenous population to have to deal with money. They had to buy corn, the basic staple of life.

The conversation turned heated when Venancio, after a few *tragos* of *aguardiente*, laid into George Bush Sr., and about the NAFTA trade agreement which really damaged the native farmers. He was really pissed off. It is unusual to see an indigenous man let off steam. This was a sight. And suddenly I became the ugly American.

I felt so disconnected from the American political scene. For a long time I had been an environmental activist, but had then directed my energy to my own pursuits. It was this highly uncomfortable wake up call from Venancio that turned my attention to what was happening with the control of the food supply.

Time came to leave the next day, and on parting, Doña Julieta said, "Let's go north and teach again." I had an instant flash. It was not to happen again.

She gave us a traditional blessing on leaving, a *limpia* with *copal* smoke. The indelible smell memory of ceremony and the *sierra*. We said goodbye to the family and left. I did not look back.

CHAPTER 36 WHEN THE TRANSLATOR BECOMES THE TEACHER – CARRYING THE BULTO

I do not believe that anyone can understand the shock to the indigenous mind witnessing the rapidity and complexity of change that overtook the *sierra*. And yet, with roads coming into the region, allowing the entrance of all kinds of things into this once quite hidden land, the magic is still strong. What occurs here, healings quite beyond explanation is a manifestation of the *Todo Poderoso* (All Powerful).

Witnessing the mysterious and powerful in nature, the occult energies, the spirits, the inter-dimensional beings, strange movements of animals and insects, the heavenly phenomena, auguries and so much more, these things like punctuation in time, exclamation points, dance in my minds eye. Knowing that there is a transmission here, something wonderful, truly that which provokes a state of wonder, gives great solace in these times of change. As the great Wheel of Time turns, the knowledge of the sacred plants becomes even more important. Ceremony is the key.

Time and time again, Doña Julieta would tell me that you only learn by living with the teacher. Doing this, the apprentice learns to serve first. Watching her delicate hands do the toughest work, even thinking of them makes me want to hold them. "*Manos frescas y curativas*" (Cool and healing hands), she would say to me with a loving look as she held mine.

In the early days being with her, I stumbled along learning

Spanish on the way. Being laughed at a lot was a real impetus to remember the vocabulary and the pronunciation. Once the stumbling was over and the language flowed, I became aware of another aspect of the responsibility that I was given. I was called on to translate many times.

Good translation is an art, and takes dominion over words and their context in order to accurately transmit the teachings. Few people consider the translator when they go for teachings. Ignored, overlooked, always taking a lower seat, in reality the translator is the teacher.

The study of a language takes a long time. Integrating to memory the technical vocabulary of various topics as well as traditional native medicine is ample. Instantaneously applying this in simultaneous translation requires a certain type of what could be likened to channeling. It is quite like a mind link with the teacher. Your integrity lies with your clear delivery. In a moment.

Doña Julieta poured the teachings into me and foretold that I should teach. On returning to Northern California, I founded the Institute of Traditional Native Medicine, Kalpulli Tonantzin and an apprenticeship program. All of my students are women.

At this time I reflect on some of my indigenous elders who I had the privilege of being with. A number of them told me that they were sad that they did not have anyone to pass on the teachings to. Many said to me that their children were not interested in learning. I have witnessed this.

Now, holding the feminine lineage of the sacred mushrooms has me thinking the same thing as some of my medicine elders now passed. Wondering where the real students are. As one ages, one recognizes the preciousness of time. There is no fast track in learning the medicine way. It all takes time.

The *bulto* (sacred bundle) that I carry is precious. The knowledge has been passed down orally. My studies have included many rare books also. Remembering the many times that I visited Tlakaelel, asking questions about the occult, he often steered me to his library. Under lock and key, he always allowed me access to his most treasured books. For me his library was holy ground. He has changed dimensions now and is sorely missed.

My own eyes are witnessing a massive change in young people with the great distraction in electronic hand held devices. Many illnesses are now arising because of electromagnetic distortions and radiation from these things. With insta-information, there is belief that everything you read on the Internet is true. Or that you can learn about anything on the Internet.

Certain kinds of music disturbing and numbing the mind with loud blasting beats, the designers doing their best to keep you numb. All kinds of things available to really mess you up. The supermarket has amplified. Brain dysfunction is rampant. Controlling forces have a choke hold on consciousness.

Yet there has arisen another part of our grand tribe, the younger open ones, with good hearts and inquisitive minds, searching like we all have. For those of you who have not lost the way of beauty, whose beings have been touched by the Great Mystery, and for those of you who wish to know essence wisdom, I hold on to my vision, and write this for you, wherever you are. Know that you are a part of this great cosmic weaving.

Todo Poderoso directs all, and it is said that those that hold the customs and ceremonies will become even more valuable as the deterioration in the external world continues. It is the kindness of the elders that continues to move me forward, walking into their footsteps. It is the call of the Mother Earth to step up our activities to protect Her. Get busy! Time is of the essence.

Initiated woman has spiritual and mental fire. In the Sierra Mazateca, the wise ones are called Eagle Warriors. There is a calling through time to other women to seek these initiatory experiences that define the shape of life. In Mexico, the ancestors left us *Flores y Cantos* (Flowers and Songs). The meaning is deep.

All my teachers left me a trail of breadcrumbs to follow. They pointed the way, many times subtly to see if I would pick up their lead. As a good student, I followed and practiced the methods. Mandatory to the effort was innumerable pilgrimages to ancient places of power, such as the many archeological sites with pyramids, where ceremony was done. Much time and effort were made to get there when the travel was rough.

We are trained in our education to ask questions. With native elder teachers, this is not such a good thing to do. Through them we learn another language. Stop talking, start listening and start observing. Or best said by one of my precious teachers, "Shut up!" No complaining about the teacher's tone of voice.

We all want things the easy way. We are very spoiled. Learning the medicine way is tough. The training moulds you into strength and makes you full of love and compassion. In as a cream puff and out as tempered steel. Through the flames time and time again. You must learn to sacrifice to get the teachings. This means that you have to give it all. You cannot hold onto anything. Physical hardship, time, money, offerings and service are of the essence. You do whatever you can. If you really want the teachings, you need to go for it!

Authentic teachers are unconventional. Expectations otherwise are futile. Many seekers jump after anyone in an exotic costume. On this note, I always recall a wonderful statement by a great Tibetan master describing these kinds of fakes, he said, "Like dog shit wrapped in brocade."

Living in indigenous reality is much more difficult than most can imagine. There is also much beauty. It is because of these tremendous challenges, that the medicine people are so very special. Like diamonds on a beach. Now planetary movement of the medicine ways is calling us to our own flowering in times of turbulent waters.

Doña Julieta one day was watching me writing. She said, "You should write books. You are an artist, you must make movies!" She was nudging me towards my destiny.

In her house hung a black and white photo portrait of Ché Guevara. Doña Julieta like many people in Latin America loved him and honored him. As I readied to leave her house she said his famous saying that she always said to us on parting, *"Hasta la Victoria Siempre!"* (Always to Victory!). She gave me a big hug. And then, she gave me a profound look with her dark eyes blazing like a wise eagle and with her last words said, "Go to the Maya! The real ones (meaning shamans) are still there!" It was a *mandado*. I was being sent on a quest.

In order to find out what happened, dear reader, read on in The Maya Chronicles.

"Treasure finders of all sorts will appear continuously,
And treasure-doctrines will pour forth like spores from mushrooms.
None of them will fail to bear fruit;
They will be reminders of me, Orgyen."

A prophecy from the treasures of Trime Kunga

<u>The Nyingma School of Tibetan Buddhism</u>,
by Dudjom Rinpoche

ABOUT THE AUTHOR

Camila Martinez, M.A. is a curandera, yogini, filmmaker, photographer, author, poet, radio producer, eco-warrior, seed mother, translator, and sustainability consultant. She is an international speaker, teacher and consultant. Apprenticing under Doña Julieta in the Sierra Mazateca, Oaxaca, Mexico for twenty years, she learned the healing ways of the sacred mushrooms for which this region is renowned. She is also the first western woman to receive a graduate degree in Ayurveda and Tibetan Medicine. A holder of several lineages, she has been adopted into numerous tribes.

She is the founder of The Institute of Traditional Native Medicine in northern California, USA. Her work has been dedicated for the benefit of indigenous people and women. For the past fifteen years she has worked intensively as the director of The Maya Seed Ark Project with the Maya in three countries on sustainability and food security, emphasizing emergency seed banks.

She has produced two films on GMOs and seed saving in Spanish and two Mayan dialects: Alarma! No a los Transgenicos, and Las Enseñanzas de las Madres de las Semillas, and the English language film The Seed Mother's Transmissions.

Practitioner of The Gift Economy, she devotes her efforts to the raising of consciousness and healing on our planet.